*The Way to Write
Crime Fiction*

The Way to Write Crime Fiction

By
LISANNE RADICE

Elm Tree Books . London

ELM TREE BOOKS

Published by the Penguin Group
27 Wrights Lane, London W8 5TZ, England
Viking Penguin Inc, 40 West 23rd Street, New York, New York 10010, U.S.A.
Penguin Books Australia Ltd, Ringwood, Victoria, Australia
Penguin Books Canada Ltd, 2801 John Street, Markham, Ontario, Canada L3R 1B4
Penguin Books (N.Z.) Ltd, 182-190 Wairau Road, Auckland 10, New Zealand

Penguin Books Ltd, Registered Offices: Harmondsworth, Middlesex, England

First published in Great Britain 1989 by
Elm Tree Books

British Library Cataloguing in Publication Data

Radice, Lisanne
   Way to write crime fiction. —
   (Way to write).
   1.   Crime fiction. Authorship
   I.   Title   II.   Series
   808.3

   ISBN 0-241-12461-1
   ISBN 0-241-12462-x Pbk

Typeset by Pioneer, Perthshire
Printed and bound in Great Britain by
Billing and Sons Ltd, Worcester

To Jane, Felicia, Janet,
Sarah and Misia

Contents

Introduction

Why do you, the potential author, and reader of this book, want to write crime fiction? Have you already thought of a plot? Do you have a particular theme you want to expand, or do you need that little bit of extra encouragement to start a book? Are you perhaps unsure what type of crime fiction you want to pursue, or do you really see yourself as a crime novelist, and are not merely interested in writing a novel with some mystery attached to it? Is your aim to amuse and entertain, or do you secretly long to produce a work with a great message at its heart? In other words, are you quite certain what writing crime fiction entails?

However, before you decide which type of crime fiction is for you, you need to consider the basic rules of crime writing. You must decide on your plot, how your characters are going to develop, the solution to your mystery. Not necessarily in great detail, but you do need to have some idea of your basic objectives. Once you have established these in your mind, and probably also on paper, then there is nothing to stop you from starting. But are you quite certain what crime fiction entails? How it has been defined? Let me quote one of the most famous crime fiction writers of the last decade, P. D. James. If you think you can accept her definition, then read on. If you want to achieve something different, then close this book and have another look at Dickens, George Eliot, E. M. Forster, and other favourite novelists.

"There will be a violent death; a limited circle of suspects all with motives, means and opportunity; false clues; and a tenable ending with a solution to the mystery which both author and reader hope will be a satisfying consummation of suspense and excitement but which the reader could himself arrive at by a process of logical deduction from revealed facts with the aid of no more luck or intuition than it is reasonable to permit to the detective himself."

This is, of course, a description for the most part of the classic detective novel, but that definition, suitably extended, will be seen to apply, at one level or another, to the different forms of crime fiction discussed in this book.

Whereas a novel need not necessarily have a plot, it must at least have a theme, as well as that satisfying mixture of interplay between characters and psychological insights. Crime fiction on the other hand, whatever the genre, has to have a plot, a suitably strong mix of problems and puzzles, and a good modicum of action. That doesn't mean to say, that the author has no need to concern himself either with insights or particular themes; a growing number of crime novels now deal specifically with both.

Apart from these various ingredients, there is one other objective which you, the future author, need to bear in mind – the main aim of crime fiction is not to instruct, but to entertain. Readers pick up crime or suspense novels, police procedurals or thrillers, because they want to be intrigued and puzzled, to be taken out of themselves. They will also expect to be provided with an abundance of clues, a variety of suspects, and some acceptable motives for the murderer and the victim; in other words, a mixture of deduction and action.

There have, of course, been different definitions of crime fiction. Jaques Barzun, Julian Symons, H. R. F. Keating, to name but a few, have produced their own version of what they believe constitutes this genre. Symons, for instance, has written mostly about what he calls the crime detective novel; Keating ranges somewhat further, going so far as to include the espionage novel in one of his critical studies. I have decided, as you can see from the chapter headings, not to be particularly exclusive, so that I can provide you with as great a range of choice as possible. It might also give you a greater opportunity to decide where your talents lie; are you more at home with a small set of characters; do the minutiae of a police procedural arouse your interests; have you perhaps always hoped to explore the murky twilight of the espionage novel?

The reading list at the end of each chapter is seen merely as a guideline to what I consider the best, or the most interesting, (not always the same thing) books to be found in that particular genre.

Let me explain the reasons for the different categories. The classical work of detective fiction has a chapter to itself, partly in order to give you some insight into the 'golden age' of the detective novel, and partly because there are still a considerable number of writers who feel most at home in this genre. The problem, as I stress later, is to persuade publishers that a market for such work still exists.

My second category is what I call the modern crime/ detective novel. The difference between the crime novel and the classical detective novel is more a question of emphasis than a substantial change in the classical formula. P. D. James and Ruth Rendell are at the moment the two most famous examples of writers using this genre, but many more crowd hard at their heels. In a sense, the modern crime novel, with its greater preoccupation with, and exploration of, themes and characters, is simply a more profound extension of the classical genre.

As I have mentioned previously, the boundaries are easily crossed. This is particularly true of suspense or psychological novels, which can also, in some forms, sit happily in the crime novel category. The work of Margaret Yorke, June Thomson, Jessica Mann, provide a good example of either 'crime' or 'suspense' novels. On the other hand, Patricia Highsmith, Celia Fremlin and a considerable number of Margaret Millar's novels, slot more comfortably into the 'suspense' or 'psychological' framework.

The police procedural and the private eye novel are easily distinguishable. One interesting new development in the latter category is the growing number of books now devoted to the female private detective. Authors such as Sarah Paretsky and Liza Cody are good examples of writers in this genre. There is more to the thriller than just pace, as readers of Dick Francis have discovered. Despite the need for fast action, surprise, mystery, and usually murder, are also vital ingredients. As these relate closely to the major elements of most crime fiction, the thriller has been included in this book. Some critics believe that the thriller is merely an extension of the crime novel, a work of crime with pace added to it. My own argument is that writers who set out to produce thrillers see themselves as writing in a particular, and different, genre.

Finally, we come to the espionage novel. There are those who see spy fiction as also standing outside the familiar traditions of the crime novel, and would argue against its inclusion in a book of this kind. I would contend, however, that it does have a place in that, despite some very different attributes, it nevertheless also has a considerable number which are to be found in the crime novel or the thriller. A good work of spy fiction will inevitably include a substantial amount of pace, suspense, murder and mystery, as in Le Carré, as well as providing the reader with a satisfying degree of intellectual problem solving.

We have now discussed the different types of crime fiction. It may be that even before you began reading this book you had already planned in which genre to write; but if not, then I hope that the descriptions of the various categories will have helped you to decide with which one you might feel most comfortable.

Some further reading:
Jaques Barzun & Wendell Hertig Taylor, *A Catalogue of Crime*. (Harper)
H. R. F. Keating, *Whodunit? A Guide to Crime, Suspense and Crime Fiction*. (Windward)
H. R. F. Keating, *Writing Crime Fiction*. (Black)
Julian Symons, *Bloody Murder. From the Detective Story to the Crime Novel*. (Faber)

Chapter One

Simple Rules

In this chapter I will discuss the main elements which make up a work of crime fiction; the plot, the motivation, and the characters. We will also deal with what I call, for want of a better description, the essential 'do's' and 'don'ts' of crime writing.

Plot

How should you, a first time writer, deal with the problem of plot? And, once you have a plot, at least in outline, how do you set about organising your writing? Do you produce chapter headings; a fairly full synopsis; or should you just take pot luck and hope that inspiration will flow?

The plot is the central pivot on which your book, whatever its nature, relies. The sealed room detective novel, the police procedural, the action packed thriller, all need to have a plot which hangs together and logically progresses from A to B, with a beginning, a middle and an end. At the same time, the reader ought to be aware of the underlying unity which links the various elements together.

This doesn't mean that a logical progression inevitably rules out the odd and the unexpected, far from it. But whatever the surprises, the twists and the sudden happenings, they still need to relate to an overall pattern. In other words, a high level of probability has to be maintained.

A synopsis is simply a mechanical device which can provide you with a useful guide once you have decided on your central theme – a journal full of jottings can produce the same effect, though it will obviously be more haphazard. But this may be how you like to work.

5

There is no doubt that the plot is crucial to any work of crime fiction, and by plot I not only mean the logical basis to your work, but also the main theme that you have in mind. So how do you set about getting ideas which you will be able to develop into the makings of a strong plot?

Much depends on how you work. It may be that you have secretly always wanted to write about the corroding effects of an over-protective love; or of the way in which small deceits can eventually lead to murder; or how revenge can be sparked off by imagined slights. In other words how some emotions, perhaps of a trifling nature, can turn into something quite different given unexpected circumstances.

You may, on the other hand, be interested in a different approach. Not so much thematic but rather one that is based on questions of personality or of career. You may have met someone with a totally opposite life style to yours, a philatelist, an actuary, a professional dog breeder, and the very novelty of their job or their interests may well have encouraged you to weave a plot around them.

Another way of finding a central theme could perhaps be based on what I might call the 'effect of surprise encounters'. An odd looking man might suddenly cross the street twice in quick succession. Why did he do that? Could he have been avoiding someone? Had he forgotten something vital? Did he look particularly fearful?

Some writers of crime fiction use everyday and familiar surroundings and explore their possibilities. For instance, now that universities are being starved of funds, departmental cuts are biting and promotion is more or less at a standstill, an academic writing crime fiction for the first time might well devise a situation where a colleague is murdered either to clear the way for promotion, or to produce the one departmental redundancy which the Vice Chancellor has demanded!

Once you feel happy with your central theme or plot, my advice is – produce a synopsis. It doesn't matter how detailed or how slight, short or long, but working out an overall scheme will provide you with a framework, however tenuous. You don't have to be a slave to your synopsis, indeed you may eventually discard it altogether, but what it will initially produce is a certain concentration of the mind. You will be able to have an over view of most of the chapters, and to discern if events follow logically one from the other, or at any rate fit into the general pattern of the book. Once you have established your general framework you will be able to look more objectively on the work as a whole.

When you are clear about the main events, then comes the moment for fleshing them out. You can do this in two ways; by establishing motivation and by providing your central characters with the background into which they fit.

Motivation

Motivation can best be described as the reason, or reasons, why the crime about which you are writing was committed. For we must assume that some crime, (usually, though not always, murder) has taken place, or will take place. Given this premise, and whatever the circumstances or the nuances of the plot, there are three basic questions which the writer has to answer – who committed the crime, how, and why. It is true that the latter question was rarely addressed by the writers of the 'golden age' of crime fiction, whose main objective was simply to provide the reader with a satisfying intellectual puzzle, but in modern crime fiction the 'why' is often the central element of the plot, with the 'who' peripheral to the action, and the 'how' seen as irrelevant. Nevertheless, whatever the genre, some deduction, and some unravelling of the threads has to occur, hopefully in a situation where the reader's attention is gripped by suspense.

Why are crimes committed? Money, blackmail, revenge, love, jealousy, these are the usually accepted motives which lie behind serious crimes, and particularly murder – for it is murder with which you will be dealing. Why murder, you may ask, why not robbery or a particularly nasty piece of fraud? Because murder is unique, it can occur in even the most apparently ordinary situations, and because it is the worst, the most unacceptable and the most unthinkable of crimes. Violent robbery, which is perhaps the nearest serious crime there is to murder, is usually presumed to be the work of hardened criminals motivated by greed and gain. A plot which has a violent robbery and nothing more, as central to the action, would be unlikely to capture the imagination, and even more important, the involvement, of the reader. It is the eruption of the unexpected in an apparently normal setting that produces the enticement.

Characters

How do you make your characters behave and speak realistically? The most useful piece of advice I can give you is, look around you, listen and observe. Try not to use your family or your closest friends as guinea pigs (unless you want to alienate them!) but watch people on buses, in cars, in queues, at dinner tables, in meetings; all these encounters can be stored away for future use. Study peoples' mannerisms and their tone of voice, try and remember any phrases that you think are worth recording, use your imagination in putting people in different situations. Keep a notebook!

Listen to the way people you meet speak. We all have different ways of expressing ourselves, some people clip their words, others are verbose, yet others never finish their sentences. If you keep a sharp ear out for the nuances of speech you will be able to produce dialogue which has an authentic ring to it. An additional word; you ought also to bear in mind that it is important that you achieve different speech rhythms without having to insert too many 'he said' or 'she said'. The reader ought to be able, at a glance, to differentiate who is speaking to whom.

It will help in the blocking in of your characters if from the start you not only give them certain mannerisms and specific characteristics of speech, but also give them a name. A Fanny is likely to be a different person to a Dinah, an Agnes will be at home in quite other surroundings to that of a Sharon.

The way people move is another important element in the building up of characters. Are there specific traits which you want to highlight? Some mannerisms which are special to them, which differentiate them from others? If you build these into your descriptions early on, then the reader will immediately be able to identify them as they appear on your canvas from time to time. I'm not suggesting that every character has to have some special idiosyncratic trait (although there is nothing to stop you having off beat characters if they have a logical role to play) but some quite normal mannerisms can create a special bond with the reader. One of your characters might like to laugh loudly, another always has to sidle into rooms, yet another frowns when faced with a problem. If you highlight these traits, then the reader will remember them and you will have what the admen rather unglamorously call a 'recognition factor'.

Background

In plotting a work of crime fiction you must always bear in mind that you have to produce an authentic background. Do not write about a place unless you have some knowledge of it. You will immediately quote H. R. F. Keating at me (who wrote his Inspector Ghote books without ever having set foot in India) but on the whole, unless you are in a class of your own, and can read maps brilliantly, my advice still stands. Also, never describe a journey from A to B unless you are sure of your route. You are certain to be found out by some reader who travels that way daily!

Notebook

Should you keep a notebook? Again, this is very much a personal decision. Many writers do. They meticulously record names, characteristics, background, main plot, sub plot, and so on. This not only helps them to keep the action on the boil, and reminds them of events which they might otherwise have overlooked, but also allows them to build up the story brick by brick. Others don't feel the need for such a meticulous approach – they will happily shuffle pieces of paper around on which they have dotted down ideas, scraps of conversation, bits of interesting background. Having moved them satisfactorily about, a pattern, they claim, often suddenly emerges.

Clues

This finally brings me to the question of clues. Of course, the way you inject your clues into the story very much depends on the type of crime fiction you have decided to write. But even with thrillers, which are more action than puzzle, you will find it essential both to present clues and to disguise them. This means that all your sub-plots also have to follow a logical pattern and fit carefully into the mainstream of the central plot.

Sometimes the reader may be given a hint of what is to come, perhaps a description of some trait of personality which will figure more prominently in the future, but because of the earlier mention will provide a more credible explanation of an unexpected or surprising action. Remember too, that as the plot has to carry the reader along, so the end must be both sudden and yet inevitable. The solution must be arrived at at the end of the book, unless you have deliberately set out to answer the question 'Why?' rather than 'Who?'

The Beginning

It is always difficult to know how to start. But with crime fiction you have to remember one golden rule – it is vital to grip your reader right from the beginning. Let me show you what I mean by quoting the following examples of first paragraphs:

"His plans had been running so beautifully, so goddamned beautifully, and now she was going to smash them all. Hate erupted and flooded through him, gripping his face with jaw-aching pressure. That was alright though: the lights were out."

These are the opening lines from Ira Levin's *A Kiss Before Dying*. The reader is immediately transported into a world of violence, sinister cunning, and duplicity. Naturally enough, he will want to know what happens next – what the plans were that have gone so badly wrong, what sort of person the narrator is, and who is the intended victim. Here is part of the opening paragraph of John Le Carré's *The Honourable Schoolboy*:

"Afterwards, in the dusty little corners where London's secret servants drink together, there was argument about where the Dolphin case history should really begin. One crowd, led by a blimpish fellow in charge of microphone transcription, went so far as to claim that the fitting date was sixty years ago when 'that arch-cad Bill Haydon' was born into the world under a treacherous star. Haydon's very name struck a chill into them. It does so even today."

A quite different beginning, but just as gripping. Treachery, mystery, the unmasking of villains, all are hinted at in the first few sentences. Finally, an excerpt from one of the most creative novelists of the twentieth century, Graham Greene; an opening paragraph from *The Third Man* which brilliantly reveals a mystery, poses a question, and introduces a dead man.

"One never knows when the blow may fall. When I saw Rollo Martins first I made this note on him for my police files. 'In normal circumstances a cheerful fool. Drinks too much and may cause a little trouble. Whenever a woman passes raises his eyes and makes some comment, but I get the impression that he'd really rather not be bothered. Has never really grown up and perhaps that accounts for the way he worshipped Lime.' I wrote that phrase 'in normal circumstances' because I met him first at Harry Lime's funeral."

The Middle
You may not find it too difficult to produce an eyecatching first paragraph, but how to keep up the momentum? The most important problem you have to face is the question of pace (crucial to all types of crime fiction), how the action can best be presented so that the moments of drama are effectively interspersed by intervals of quiet which, though not dull, neatly lead up to the next dramatic event. In other words, you must learn to find a balance between the sudden twists to the story and the linkage passages. There are different ways round this problem: a minor character can be introduced, some interesting dialogue can take place, a character may suddenly muse on the past. Then can come your sudden twist, unexpected yet somehow inevitable, and the story will once more move briskly forward.

The End
The end might seem obvious in a work of crime fiction – the murderer is unmasked and, usually, brought to justice.

Certainly, the solution to the puzzle must produce a satisfactory ending. It must have what Keating has called a 'happy' outcome. The reader will expect it.

Do's and Don'ts

Finally, some do's and don'ts. *Do* read widely, particularly the type of crime fiction in which you intend to specialise. Look carefully at how the author has constructed the plot, how that happy blend of action and description is achieved, and how the dialogue reflects the traits of the main characters.

Do get your facts right, not only about the background, but also about general police procedures; note the hierarchical nature of the police force, and how criminal courts work. *Do* spend perhaps a day in a Crown Court or a magistrates court; they each have a different atmosphere which is particular to them, and which you ought to understand if you intend using either in your story.

Do see that your forensic information is correct, if that's what you're going to rely on as part of your plot. Certain poisons have certain characteristics – get them right. Do you know enough about finger printing to produce a credible description? Sound knowledge of your subject is essential here.

Don't have long descriptions which hold up the story, and add nothing to the action. *Don't* allow your characters to launch themselves into a lengthy narrative which will only bore the reader. *Don't* forget that dialogue has to be lively and add to the pace; long monologues simply act as a break on the action.

Finally, remember that the publishers will be looking for a book of about 65 to 80,000 words; anything below or above will have far greater difficulty in being accepted. Apart from the fun of writing a book, you should also remind yourself that you want to see it in print!

Chapter Two

The Classical Whodunit

In this chapter I intend to discuss classical detective fiction, or the locked room mystery story. This genre, as we have seen, reached its peak in the nineteen thirties and forties – the era of the four grand dames of the detective saga, Agatha Christie, Dorothy L. Sayers, Margery Allingham, and Ngaio Marsh, as well as John Dickson Carr, Rex Stout and Nicholas Blake.

Since then, it must be admitted, it has been superceded by the detective novel. That doesn't mean to say that if you are particularly hooked on the classical form or that you have an intricate plot for a murder complete with an intriguing group of suspects and a charismatic detective to solve it, you shouldn't give it a try; but be warned, publishers will be difficult to convince.

Let me remind you of the main characteristics of this type of crime fiction: it is seen first and foremost as light entertainment, but an entertainment which relies upon the reader's interest in a logical pursuit of clues honestly put before him; the hero is the, usually, amateur detective who by his intellectual brilliance, and through a process of ratiocination, is able to deduce the character of the murderer from among the small number of people who make up the cast of possible suspects.

The setting is often a small country house, (maps of the surroundings are even sometimes provided), and the characters are seen more in terms of motives than as people in their own right. In other words, there is a certain element of the static in the classic crime story.

Perhaps the best way to demonstrate the above is to quote

from Ronald Knox's *Decalogue*, which was a list of rules he suggested should be kept in mind by detective writers, and which first appeared in the Preface to *Best Detective Stories of 1928-29.*

1. The Criminal must be someone mentioned in the early part of the story, but must not be anyone whose thoughts the reader has been allowed to follow.

2. All Supernatural or preternatural agencies are ruled out as a matter of course.

3. Not more than one secret room or passage is allowable.

4. No hitherto undiscovered poisons may be used, nor any applicance which will need a long scientific explanation at the end.

5. No Chinaman must figure in the story.

6. No accident must ever help the detective, nor must he ever have an unaccountable intuition which proves to be right.

7. The detective must not himself commit the crime.

8. The detective must not light on any clues which are not instantly produced for the inspection of the reader.

9. The Stupid Friend of the detective, the Watson, must not conceal any thoughts which pass through his mind; his intelligence must be slightly, but very slightly, below that of the average reader.

10. Twin Brothers, and doubles generally, must not appear unless we have been duly prepared for them.

The main inference is that the writer has to play fair and produce logical clues. There is also however another underlying assumption which is, that the reader is not expected to become involved in the characters portrayed; that it is the plot which is important and not those around whom the plot is centred. You can see why today's publishers are less than keen on this type of crime fiction. But you

14

never know, the fashion may change, and the golden classics (which are after all still read in their millions) may stage a comeback.

So just to keep all options open, let us look at some of the best examples of the genre and see if we can learn anything from them.

Apart from the plot, the most important ingredient of the classic detective story is the detective. What are the characteristics of these larger than life heroes? What do Hercule Poirot, Lord Peter Wimsey, Maigret, Albert Campion, John Appleby have in common?

First, they are immediately memorable, extremely intelligent and with a penchant for quick thinking and the sharp repartee. Secondly, they sometimes have a Watson trailing behind them, full of admiration, somewhat credulous, but providing the perfect foil to the razor sharp mentality of their mentor.

Hercule Poirot has his Hastings, Campion has the unfortunate Lugg, and Holmes of course has the indomitable Watson. To give you a flavour of the usefulness of the appreciative supporter let me quote from one of Sherlock Holmes' most famous conversations:

Watson: Is there any other point to which you would wish to draw my attention?
Holmes: To the curious incident of the dog in the night-time.
Watson: The dog did nothing in the night-time.
Holmes: That was the curious incident.

In four short sharp sentences Conan Doyle is able to demonstrate his detective's superiority, move the story along, and titillate the reader by providing a clear pointer to the unravelling of the mystery.

Margery Allingham uses her Watson in a quite different way. Lugg is depicted as the archetypal buffoon whose unsavoury comments highlight the aristocratic bearing of his employer, and whose lumbering remarks inject a note of casual chaos.

Mr Lugg, Mr Campion's 'male-person's gentleman', regarded his employer with reproachful little black eyes.

15

"You 'eard," he said, and added with charming confiding, "I was cleanin' meself up. You'd do well to put on a dressing-gown and a belt."

"A belt?" inquired Campion, taken off his guard.

"Braces is low, except when worn with a white waistcoat for billiards."

Lugg made the pronouncement with justifiable pride. "I picked that up down at the club today. You'll 'ave to get a new robe too. Mr Tuke's young feller has a different-coloured one for every day of the week. What do you say to that idea?"

"Slightly disgusting."

Sweet Danger

Simenon has yet another approach. Although his Inspector Maigret quite often finds himself in a locked room situation he has no need of a Watson, his approach is psychological; Maigret is more interested in situations than in the finding of clues. The following extract gives some flavour of what Simenon was trying, with great success, to achieve.

'The Chief Inspector was led to a first-floor room where mosquitoes immediately started to buzz round his head. He was in a bad temper. The job on hand was a dull one, unexciting and very ordinary.

Nevertheless, once in bed, instead of going to sleep, he began to see pictures of Gallet, sometimes only his cheek, sometimes the lower part of his face.

He kept tossing and turning in the damp sheets. He could hear the river's babble as it lapped against the sandbanks.

Each criminal case has its own special features, which you stumble on sooner or later, and which often hold the key to the mystery.

Perhaps the special feature of this one was that everything was ordinary.'

Maigret Stonewalled

Having established the character of your detective and the ambience in which he works, you then need to produce the serious crime – usually a murder which he or she has to investigate. How do you present that murder to your readers?

You might start by asking yourself three simple questions: Where in the story is the murder committed? If it is more than a quarter of the way through the book, then the chances

16

are you're writing a suspense novel rather than classical crime fiction.

Is the method of murder eye-catching, either in the way it is presented, or the circumstances surrounding the crime.

And finally, whatever your method of murder, is it believable? The victim must never be killed in such a way that the reader will feel he has been cheated.

If you follow these three very simple rules you won't go far wrong.

So, now what about the clues? We have seen from Ronald Knox's somewhat tongue in the cheek list that, given the presumption of a locked room mystery, the characters will be expected eventually to give themselves away either by what they say, or what they omit to say; what they do or don't do. The clues must be presented fairly to the reader, very much as they would be to the detective.

How does the crime writer set about planting clues as honestly as possible, in such a way that unless the reader is very sharp he or she will find themselves unwittingly accepting and not questioning what is put before them. Remember, you have agreed that you will not cheat. But how to baffle?

First of all make sure that you produce enough legitimate clues as to the murderer's identity. It is not enough to provide just one, obscurely hidden in the middle of the book. A good way of presenting clues and yet hiding them is to have a scene in which a long list is put before the reader, one of the items being the relevant clue. Dorothy L. Sayers, in a much quoted passage from her book *Five Red Herrings* lists all the paints which a painter has recently been using on his canvas. Hidden among the items is a paint which could not have been used. Because the list is long the reader will probably have skimmed through it on the assumption that a merely rather tedious enumeration of the paraphernalia of painting has nothing to do with the solution of the crime.

Another kind of list is for the detective to notice, though in passing, certain characteristics of all the members of the household to whom he talks. He might, for instance, idly speculate on the different types of finger nails of the various suspects; some are bitten to the quick, some have nail polish peeling off them, others are clean, yet others are over long and so on. If the murder has taken place in the garden during a heavy rain storm, then the fact that one of the suspects has particularly clean hands might make the detective note their pristine state – but this need not be taken up until much later in the book.

A second method of producing baffling evidence is to announce loudly the finding of what is seen as an apparently vital clue. Agatha Christie is particularly good at producing clues which basically muddy the waters. A bloody hand-kerchief is found among the contents of a secret drawer in one of the suspect's rooms. The inference is obvious – he or she has something to hide. Three chapters on we find that the handkerchief has nothing to do with the crime which has just been committed, it simply gives us an insight into that person's background.

This brings me onto what one might call 'association' clues. The first type is when the author produces a clue which leads the reader to presume certain consequences. The suspect is described as ill, or even shot, in any case in no fit state to have committed the crime. But if you look at the text closely at no time is it ever made clear that they really were shot or, though in bed, unable to get up.

The second type of 'association' clue is what H. R. Keating has called the clue of deception. Except that it's not. The example he gives is as follows: "We are told on unimpeach-able authority that a woman is looking forward to the birth of her daughter; years later we read of a young man arriving on the scene. So we do not think, 'Ah, this is the mother's child.' Our response to talk of the birth of a daughter is that a daughter was born, provided of course that the talk and the child are separated by a long period of time and a reasonable number of pages."

There is a third type of 'association' clue which is difficult to pull off as readers can feel cheated. This is to make the obvious suspect, say the big bully, or the unpleasant petty crook, who the reader will not suspect (because he presumes the author far too devious) end up as the murderer. As you can imagine, you have to treat this type of situation rather carefully. You will have to produce other suspects who the reader perhaps would not want to have committed the crime, so that it is eventually with something like relief that he discovers that after all it was the unpleasant character who was the villain. Let me now give you four very straightforward examples of how Agatha Christie set about describing her hero-detective, how she apparently pinpoints obvious suspects; seems to lift suspicion from the person who eventually turns out to be the murderer, and produces a useful red herring; all major ingredients of the classic work of crime fiction. The first three are taken from *Murder in Mesopotamia*, published in 1936, the last from *Death on the Nile* which came out one year later.

The narrator describes her first sight of Hercule Poirot:

"I don't know what I'd imagined — something rather like Sherlock Holmes — long and lean with a keen, clever face. Of course I knew he was a foreigner, but I hadn't expected him to be *quite* as foreign as he was, if you know what I mean.

When you saw him you just wanted to laugh! He was like something on the stage or at the pictures. To begin with he wasn't above five-foot five, I should think — an odd plump little man, quite old, with an enormous moustache, and a head like an egg. He looked like a hairdresser in a comic opera."

Here the author presents a memorable description of Hercule Poirot whose vital disguise is his foreignness. From this it logically follows that no right minded Britisher need take him seriously. She therefore produces a situation where the suspects, underestimating their opponent, provide him with a perfect cover with which to solve the crime.

The second example deals with a vital ingredient of the 'locked room' mystery. Various members of the household where the murder has been committed refuse to accept that any of them can be under suspicion. The different suspects suggest that the crime was the work of some 'outsider', but this is immediately refuted by Hercule Poirot, who tells them that the murderer could only have come from among the group.

"Mr Mercado stood up too. His hands were shaking and his eyes were bloodshot.

19

'I agree. It is an outrage — an insult —'

'No, no,' said Mr Poirot. 'I do not insult you. I merely ask you all to face facts. *In a house where murder has been committed, every inmate comes in for a certain share of suspicion.* I ask you what evidence is there that the murderer came from outside at all?'"

And yet the murder occurred at a time when apparently everyone had an alibi. In this third example we find Agatha Christie seemingly establishing that no one could possibly have gone into the room where the murder took place, presenting the reader with the undoubted phenomenon of a 'locked room' mystery.

"David Emmott spoke clearly and concisely in his pleasant soft American voice.

'I was working with the pottery from a quarter to one till a quarter to three — overseeing the boy Abdullah, sorting it, and occasionally going up to the roof to help Dr Leidner.'

'How often did you go up to the roof?'

'Four times, I think.'

'For how long?'

'Usually a couple of minutes — not more. But on one occasion after I'd been working a little over half an hour I stayed as long as ten minutes — discussing what to keep and what to fling away.'

'And I understand that when you came down you found the boy had left his place?'

'Yes. I called him angrily and he reappeared from outside the archway. He had gone out to gossip with the others.'

'That was the only time he left his work?'

'Well, I sent him up once or twice to the roof with pottery.'

Poirot said gravely: 'It is hardly necessary to ask you, Mr Emmott, whether you saw anyone enter or leave Mrs Leidner's room during this time?'

Mr Emmott replied promptly.

'I saw no one at all. Nobody even came out into the court-yard during the two hours I was working.'"

This is one of the central passages of the book, and if you intend to produce classical crime fiction you will need to establish just such clues and red herrings. In fact, what the author has done here is apparently to demonstrate that no one could have gone into the victim's room without being seen, but at the same time, as we learn later, she has also provided us with a vital clue as to the identity of the murderer and how he in fact, could, and did, kill his wife.

My last example is taken from *Death on the Nile* which is also full of clues cleverly planted as well as cleverly disguised. The following excerpt shows the red herring technique.

The victim is a young and beautiful millionairess recently married to someone who appears to adore her. Here he is, (in fact he turns out to be the murderer) telling Hercule Poirot about his wife's background.

"Her father was only just ordinary plain wealthy, but after his marriage he naturally began playing the markets or whatever you call it. And as a result of that, of course, several people got it in the neck. Well, I gather there was someone on board whose father had got up against Linnet's father and taken a pretty hard knock. I remember Linnet saying: 'It's pretty awful when people hate you without even knowing you.'"

The reader immediately begins to rack his brains as to who that 'someone' is. And, of course, that 'someone' has never existed.

We have now dealt with the detective, the murder, and the clues. All of these are the backbone of the plot, which is the unravelling of the mystery. There is one final element in the classical work of crime fiction which we need to look at, and that is the denouement.

How do the great writers of classical crime fiction set about unmasking their villains? Here, as with the other ingredients, a definite tradition was established. The suspects are all lined up in front of the detective, who then proceeds to demonstrate that a case can be made against most of them, but that there is, despite all the evidence, just one of them who is the murderer. He shows off his powers of logical deduction, pinpoints the clues which, despite close attention to the text, the reader has missed, and accepts the congratulations of either the remaining suspects, or, as in some cases, his Dr Watson. It is of course an even more brilliant achievement if you have, like Rex Stout's detective, Nero Wolfe, not moved out of your study.

Here is how Michael Innes introduces the unmasking. It comes from his book, *A Night of Errors*. John Appleby, having listened to one theory as to who the murderer could be, steps in.

'Again Appleby shook his head. It might almost have been supposed that he was embarrassed. "That's not quite it," he said. "It's rather that your whole reconstruction needs dismantling and fresh disposition in a different basis. Some quite big things must be brought in — like the tramp. And some quite little ones — like Sir Oliver Dromio's vanity — what I have called his fastidiousness in the matter of ties . . . Still, you have got the case to a very definite point." Appleby paused. "But it's the point to which the criminal designed that you should get it."

And he then proceeds to unravel the plot.
Ngaio Marsh leads the reader on even more obviously.

"Well?" he said. "What do you want to know?"
"Everything," said Nigel.
"All right. Lay back your ears. Here goes."
He pulled forward a couple of dingy arm chairs and rolled back the doors of the dock, letting in a thin flood of sunshine.
"Here goes," he repeated and, lighting a cigarette, began his discourse.' *Enter a Murderer*

So there you have the classic whodunit. If you think you have found a brilliantly inventive plot which will tease your readers' imagination and provide them with the scope to use their powers of logical deduction then don't hesitate, start mapping out your synopsis! And you never know, you might strike lucky and find a publisher who is still intrigued by the genre, or they may even have a second flowering! You can always point to the fact that the great writers are still among the most popular of all crime books borrowed from public libraries.

Further Reading
Margery Allingham *Flowers for the Judge* (Heinemann)
Nicholas Blake *The Case of the Abominable Snowman* (Collins)

John Dickson Carr *The Crooked Hinge* (Hamish Hamilton)
Agatha Christie *The Murder of Roger Ackroyd* (Collins)
Rex Stout *The League of Frightened Men* (Collins)
Ngaio Marsh *Singing in the Shrouds* (Cassell)

Chapter Three

The Crime/Detective novel

The crime novel has come a long way. A greater freedom for the crime writer has been achieved in that writers now feel able to pursue any theme with which they are most comfortable. You can, like Peter Dickinson, establish a world of extraordinary fantasy; or like Julian Symons set out to show the violence behind respectable faces; or as Nicholas Freeling did with his unorthodox detective Van der Valk, meticulously strip bare the suburban pretensions of a capital city. Whatever the objective, that freedom has ensured that the new parameters of the crime novel not only encourage a greater flexibility, but also enable writers to produce work which, as with P. D. James and Barbara Vine, at its best ranks equal with more 'literary' output.

One of the major problems of the classical work of detective fiction was the rigidity of the structure. Characters were not expected to develop into personalities, while the 'closed room' scenario admitted to no extra imaginative touches. The logical and careful deduction of clues was seen as the essential heart of the story. This somewhat narrow and restricted format produced too many stereotypes, with the result that the more talented writers began to break out of the formula in order to produce what we now call crime or detective novels.

What the new generation of writers have done is to shift the emphasis from the dry accumulation of clues and their unravelling by the hero/detective, to a more subtle and broader characterisation of those caught up in the drama of the murder. The writing of both crime and detective novels now relies on a subtlety and imaginative approach lacking in the work of previous practitioners.

What is the difference between a crime and a detective novel? I have married the two together simply because the ingredients tend to be the same, with the one exception that in the detective novel the hero or heroine is the old fashioned detective brought up to date. That 'appeal to curiosity, wonder and the love of ingenuity' which Barzun describes, remains the same. But the emphasis has changed – the book now deals more with a puzzle of character than a puzzle of motive and opportunity. And of course, some of the basic rules remain; there has to be a crime and its perpetrator has to be brought out into the open. But now it is the unveiling of the different layers of personality that lies at the root of the plot, rather than a question of clever, logical deduction. The crime is not so much looked upon as an ingenious method of murder whose deduction will provide a satisfactory intellectual puzzle, but rather as needing to be understood through the behaviour of the main protagonists. It is crucial to establish, in the case of the detective novel, a strong personality, a detective who has distinctive and immediately recognisable qualities, and whose background and private life are of as much consequence as is the solving of the murder. The plot should be based not only on the process of deduction but also on a thematic linkage of the main personalities. Clues therefore become less important, insight crucial. These attributes are common to both the crime and the detective novel.

The gradual evolution of characters now becomes the main focus of the plot, with the background used as a means of building up tensions which are later revealed.

As Keating has persuasively argued in his book on the writing of crime fiction, the important difference between a detective story and a detective novel is that, whereas the former relies on a straightforward storyline based on the deduction of clues, the latter not only has depth of character, but also, and this is where the two really part company, it has a theme. Hatred, love, jealousy, meanness, each in its time has been seen as the underlying concept on which a crime novel has been based.

Once you have decided on your theme, and it is important

that you should do this right at the beginning, then that underlying emotion will, you will find, produce its own logical impetus. Someone who is jealous will behave differently to someone who is a miser.

How does the inclusion of a theme change the nature of the writing? First, it adds a new perspective to the characters. They act in a certain way because they have certain characteristics peculiar to them; certain emotions cause them to do different things. Given this new dimension, then the reason why such and such a personality has become the victim of a murder can be deduced from the reactions which they cause the murderer to feel. The logic of this approach is to show, not only the character of the murderer but also the victim, as crucial to the unwinding of the mystery. This deep involvement with the protagonists in the drama has moved the crime novel much nearer the straight novel than was ever previously thought possible.

If the motives and personalities of the murderer and the victim have become an essential ingredient of the crime/ detective novel, the personality of the detective has become paramount. It is he or she whose insights into their own, and other, lives, produces the solution to the puzzle. It is their ability to project themselves into the minds of those around them which enables them to understand underlying motives.

Which writers should the aspiring author look to for examples of best practice? Perhaps the most famous at the moment are P. D. James, Ruth Rendell, H. R. F. Keating, Julian Symons, Nicholas Freeling, Colin Dexter, Peter Dickinson, Michael Gilbert, Reginald Hill, but there are many more who could just as easily be mentioned. P. D. James, with her detective poet Dalgleish, a quirky widower and perceptive assessor of situations has become more and more interested in character and emotions than in the pursuit of clues; Ruth Rendell's Wexford, a man with family problems, humane and understanding of the young, is now in competition with her much more ambitious work published under the name of Barbara Vine; Colin Dexter's Inspector Morse, sometimes blundering, easily put on to the wrong scent, is very much an original, while Reginald Hill's team of Dalziell, fat, coarse and unloved, and Pascoe his number two, clever, introspective and over sensitive, provide a brilliant, and highly complex foil for each other. As to Peter Dickinson, he is in a class of his own; his world is a world of fantasy, of improbable conjecture, and yet one which is entirely plausible.

What is clear from the above is that the detective is more likely now to be a professional policeman than a brilliant amateur, and that the essential unravelling of the mystery will depend on the daily slog of detective work rather than on the sudden flashes of a genius like intuition.

Let us look at a very straightforward, very classical detective novel, Colin Dexter's *The Silent World of Nicholas Quinn*. Each of Colin Dexter's books are a puzzle, with clever and intricate plots, an eccentric detective, and a mild, though sometimes critical, subordinate. His Detective Chief Inspector Morse revels in solving crossword puzzles, is admired by his colleagues despite occasional lapses of bad temper, and sees each murder case as a puzzle whose pieces have to be slotted neatly into each other. This use of the puzzle element means that Morse is able to produce solutions which are then often discarded until the final, and usually surprising, truth is revealed. In *The Silent World of Nicholas Quinn* the interest lies in the way in which the author exploits the victim's deafness as the cause of his death. The theme is greed and innocence, the greed of two men who, by chance, are unmasked by a man whose naivety and innocence brings about his own murder. A juxtaposition of good and evil.

If we dissect *The Silent World of Nicholas Quinn*, more closely, it bears a considerable resemblance to the blueprint novels of the great classical tradition – but it has moved many steps forward, despite having, at its heart the very same logical approach to clues, a more or less closed list of suspects, and the same sudden and brilliant deduction which hinges on a single mistake (meticulously signalled early on in the book) made by the victim. It is the subtlety, the interest in the victim, seen as a rounded personality, which differentiates the Dexter book from that of the novels of the 1930s. Writing from the victim's viewpoint at the start of the book adds an extra dimension to the plot; bonds the reader more closely to the action, and allows the victim's personality and characteristics to provide the motive for the murder. Intelligently used it can be a powerful weapon for the author.

The reader's sympathy and curiosity, is engaged from the start:

"Yes, Quinn was enjoying his new job. It was only the phones that caused him trouble and (he admitted it) considerable embarrassment. There were two of them in each office: a white one for internal extensions, and a grey one for outside calls. And there they sat, squat and menacing, on the right hand side of Quinn's desk as he sat writing; and he prayed they wouldn't ring, for he was still unable to quell the panic which welled up within him whenever their muted, distant clacking compelled him to lift up one or other (he never knew which)."

A few sentences later comes the initial clue, presented fairly to the reader.

"He locked the papers away . . . and allowed himself to wonder whether Monica would be going for a drink or a sandwich at the Horse and Trumpet — a pub he had originally misheard as the 'Whoreson Strumpet'."

The introduction of Morse, the Inspector who deals with the murder is subtly intriguing:

"Morse looked directly into the long mirror in front of him, and there surveyed the reflection of the smaller hand mirror held behind him, in which, in turn, he considered the occipital regions of what he liked to think of as a distinguished skull."

Morse is, in fact, having a haircut.

The effect is that the reader, as in all detective stories, sees the unravelling of the plot through the eyes of the chief inspector, who is not presented as a man brilliantly in control, logically deducing clues as they appear, but someone who is often incorrect in his deductions, who has his faults, and is portrayed as a very human personality;

"Morse made two phone calls, combed his hair again, and felt inordinately happy."

28

The case is a classic one of poisoning, and the suspects, the colleagues of the victim, are paraded in front of Morse and the reader. At the same time the latter is also presented with a major clue, (unknown to the Inspector) of the successful sitting of an examination by an Arab sheik's son in his father's sheikdom.

As the chief inspector talks to all the potential murderers, each is presented so vividly that it is perfectly possible to imagine that anyone of them could have poisoned Quinn. Finally, after putting the wrong man in prison, Morse suddenly understands why the murder was committed, why people lied in order to protect a man they rightly thought innocent, and how the apparent inconsistencies of time could be resolved. There is more than one murderer. As you can see, a book written very much in the tradition of classical crime fiction, but one whose approach enlarges the earlier restrictive horizons.

P. D. James has, over the years, developed her poet, the sympathetic, private, Commander Adam Dalgleish into one of the most famous of English detectives. Her fame has rested not only on her literary craftmanship but also both on the way that her plots have developed, and the manner in which she has presented her clues. She is a very literate writer, delighting in interesting and often meticulous descriptions which remain in the memory long after the book has been returned to the shelf. The depth of her characterisation, another element which has enabled her to remain at the top of her profession, is seen at its best advantage in *A Taste for Death*.

The theme is love, its lack, insecurity and loneliness. The opening paragraphs capture the mood of the novel, demonstrating P. D. James' careful attention to even the most minor of her characters.

"Father Barnes was sitting bolt upright in his chair, his eyes staring ahead at the gleaming curve of the apse, his body taut and contracted, like that of a patient expecting pain, willing himself to endure . . . There came from him a smell, half-musty, half disagreeably sweet, of old clothes and incense, overlaid with stale sweat, a smell which was a pitiable amalgam of failure and fear."

Or the description of the police pathologist, Miles Kynaston, whose attitude to death reflects that of the author.

"Certainly, he had a taste for death. Nothing about it disconcerted him; its messiness, its smell, the most bizarre of its trappings. Unlike most doctors, he saw it, not as the final enemy but as a fascinating enigma, each cadaver, which he would gaze at with the same intent look as he must once have fixed on his living patients, a new piece of evidence which might, if rightly interpreted, bring him closer to its central mystery."

The plot is many faceted, the interrogation and unravelling of the clues divided between Adam Dalgliesh and the new woman inspector on his special team, Kate Miskin. The action moves from the family of one of the murdered men, an ex Minister of the Crown, to members of the congregation of the church where he was found, to his mistress, back to the family problems of Kate, and finally, through the many twists and convolutions of the plot, arrives at the murderer. The author makes no attempt to hide who it is, he is revealed three quarters of the way through the book, while the final pages of the novel are devoted to both the why-dun-it aspect of the crime and Adam Dalgleish's determination to break the murderer's alibi.

Motive, as we have seen, plays a major part in the new classical crime fiction genre. Here is P. D. James describing the motivation behind the murderer's actions.

"So he had it at last, the motive not only for murder but for this particular murder with its mixture of planning and impulse, its brutality, its over-ingenuity, the cleverness which hadn't quite been clever enough. It was there before him in its pettiness, its arrogance, its essential inadequacy, but in all its terrible strength. He recognised the mind behind it . . . the mind of a killer . . . who wants his victim not only dead but disgraced, the mind of a man who has felt despised and inferior all his life but who will never feel inferior again."

P. D. James therefore also uses all the ingredients of the classical formula but adds a further dimension. Her sharpness of eye as to character, her subtle gift for dialogue, her ability to move the action along in a surprising and often unconventional manner, all contribute to put her in the forefront of writers of contemporary crime fiction.

If P. D. James is the most famous example of the writer of the modern classical detective novel, Ruth Rendell matches her in the field of the crime novel. Until recently her best known work has been associated with the Wexford series, her chief Superintendent who lives in a medium sized town called Kingsmarkham and who, like Adam Dalgleish, is seen as a sensitive, but more down to earth, detective.

One of the most impressive characteristics of Ruth Rendell's writing is that it comes in many forms. There are her suspense novels, such as the brilliantly macabre *A Demon in My View*, (discussed in a later chapter) there are the Barbara Vine books, *A Dark Adapted Eye* and *A Fatal Inversion*, for which she has won the Crime Writers Golden Dagger Award, and then there are the Chief Inspector Wexford novels. All the books in the Wexford series have the same carefully constructed central plot, occasionally obscured or heightened by sub-plots which run parallel to it. Wexford's tolerance and imaginative approach to both victim and criminal are always sympathetically portrayed. In *The Veiled One*, her latest book, the theme, a strong element in the Rendell novels, is reflected in the title. Characters such as the Sanders family, a grotesque mother and a confused son, secretive and apparently unable to function in the real world, unsuccessfully attempt to hide their flawed personalities. They are not alone in their instability and their delusions. The characters, as well as the plot, as ever in a Ruth Rendell novel, are beautifully crafted.

In her Barbara Vine novels Ruth Rendell shows far less interest in the who-dun-it aspect of the crime than in the motives of her characters — though, as with all professionals, she always leaves the reader satisfied as to the evidence and the clues. In both *A Dark Adapted Eye* and *A Fatal Inversion* the background provides a major theme of the novel. In the former Rendell writes of the forgotten world of the fifties, when convention still dictated how people felt they ought to appear to the outside world, and where the genteelly respectable couldn't afford to reveal secrets which might cause them to become social pariahs. The only way to preserve old fashioned Victorian virtues seems finally, to be murder. The plot hinges on the interplay of the characters whose complex motives are gradually revealed in a brilliantly inventive piece of writing. The claustrophobic world of the small village gradually unfolds, as two sisters, Eden and Vera, each claiming to be the mother of the young Jamie, fight to keep him for themselves.

The following paragraph encapsulates some of the mood of hypocrisy which runs throughout the book. The story is told by Faith, niece of the sisters, who stays with them as a refugee from the bombings in London. Vera, writing to Faith's father, is staying with Eden who has refused to allow Jamie to return to her sister's home where, until recently, he has been brought up.

"Eden has been kindness itself, tho' I know you will agree that any other behaviour from her would have surprised us . . . It will be nice to spend some time under the same roof with him."

The author then comments

"These lines are a masterpiece of their kind for concealing true facts and real feelings. They are also perhaps a sop to Providence or a placating of the Furies. If I put a brave face on things, if I make believe all is well, all will be well."

Here is Vera, snobbishly ticking off her niece:

"The next time I called Vera 'auntie', she said in an embarrassed way that 'aunt' might sound better. Would I try to get in the way of calling her 'Aunt Vera' as 'auntie' was rather vulgar."

It is Vera who eventually stabs her sister to death.

These small vignettes produce a rich and complex texture to the book which completely grips the imagination of the reader, despite the fact that we know who committed the crime quite early on.

In *A Fatal Inversion* the same kind of technique is used as in *A Dark Adapted Eye*. Here too, the story is portrayed in a series of flashbacks, though in this case the scene shifts from

32

one character's view of past events to that of another. Again it is the background, elegiacally described, which forms the heart of the plot. This time it is the long hot summer of 1976. A group of disparate young people somehow find themselves camping in a manor house (which they romantically call Ecalpemos) recently inherited by one of them. Ten years later, the new owners of the house discover the body of a woman and a baby buried in an animal cemetery on the edge of the wood. As the complicated plot unfolds, and the different characters reveal themselves, so the reader is left in suspense both as to what really happened and why. The clues are carefully and meticulously planted.

As a sense of doom begins to emerge, so does the personality of the three main characters.

"The things that had happened to Ecalpemos, Adam resisted thinking about. He dreamed of them, he could not expel them from his unconscious mind, and they also came back to him by association, but he never allowed himself to dwell on them, to operate any random access techniques, or eye for long the mental screen where options appeared. When the process began . . . he had taught himself to touch an escape key, rather like that on the computers he sold."

One of the young people is an Indian medical student.

"He began to smile from exactly the motive Adam had attributed to him, a desire to ingratiate and to defend himself, to turn away wrath. He had been born in England, had never seen India, spoke English as his cradle tongue and had forgotten all the Hindi he had ever learned but he had all the immigrant's protective reactions and all his self-consciousness. Indeed, he had more, he thought, since the events at Ecalpemos. Things had got worse since then. There had been a gradual slow decline in his fortunes, his fate, his happiness and his prosperity, or prospect of prosperity."

And finally there is Rufus the gynaecologist.

"The half hour was spoilt but Rufus, just the same, was a disciplined man. He had not got where he was at the age of 33 by giving way to pointless speculation and neurotic inner enquiry. To have

33

recovered as he had done, so successfully, so brilliantly, after such a traumatic experience, had been a considerable feat. He had subjected himself to his own personal therapy, requiring himself to sit alone in a hospital room and speak of those happenings aloud."

Ruth Rendell's latest crime novels could very well be categorised as straight fiction, but this would be incorrect. Her stories deal not only with crime but, unlike a 'pure' novel with a body in it, they also rely on the principal characteristics of crime fiction — the need to provide clues, the why-dun-its and the how-dun-its of the genre. If the approach is different, the objectives remain the same.

However, the emphasis has changed. The new crime writers not only set out to unmask the victim's murderer, but also to peel away the protective layers of the personalities caught up in the drama of the crime. It is this new, and crucial dimension that lies at the heart of the modern crime novel.

Suggested reading:
Michael Gilbert *Smallbone Deceased* (Hodder & Stoughton)
Nicholas Freeling *The King of the Rainy Country* (Gollancz)
Julian Symons *The Colour of Murder* (Collins)
June Thomson *Not One of Us* (Constable)
Ruth Rendell *No More Dying Then* (Hutchinson)
Peter Dickinson *The Last House Party* (Bodley Head)

Chapter Four

The Suspense Novel

The suspense novel is sometimes also called the psychological novel. It is also true to say that it is often difficult to distinguish the difference between a crime and a suspense novel. All one can say is that the former, as we have seen, usually has a crime, a murder, central to the main plot, while the suspense novel need not necessarily deal with an actual crime, but can merely hint at it.

What differentiates the suspense novel, according to one well known writer, (Jessica Mann) from other crime fiction, 'resides in the intention of the author and the expectation of the reader.' The purpose of the author is to provide an unemotional dissection of both the passion and the crime which that passion has produced. The aim of the author is to illustrate the jealousies, the violence, the greed which lie behind the every day facade which people present to the outside world. This juxtaposition of normality and underlying passion produces, in the best suspense novels, an uneasy feeling of tension, of veiled menace, as ordinary dull lives reveal madness and instability.

Jessica Mann enlarges on her theme in *Whodunnit A Guide to Crime, Suspense and Spy Fiction, edited by H. R. F. Keating* by reminding us what suspense novels are not. They are not, she argues, thrillers, though some may be. They do not necessarily have to have dramatic pace, though some do. They are not mysteries, for very often the reader knows about the crime from the beginning. It is the way in which the plot unfolds that holds the reader's attention. Menace, as in some of Celia Fremlin and Margaret Yorke novels, can even be the only ingredient.

Patricia Highsmith, the most famous of suspense writers, has herself written a book on the plotting and writing of suspense fiction. What are her main suggestions?

First, she makes much of the need and importance of nurturing any ideas that may suddenly come to you, even though you may later discard them; for that you need a notebook. Ideas for stories, whether complex or trivial, slight or structured, should never be discarded; they might well come in useful on another occasion.

Once you have an idea that you are happy with then the next stage is to flesh it out with characters, with a particular background, which of itself will produce your atmosphere. However, she goes on to counsel, don't stick to a rigid plot — a flexible one gives the writer far greater possibilities.

Highsmith believes that a suspense writer "should throw some light on his character's mind; he should be interested in justice or the absence of it in the world we live in; he should be interested in the morality, good or bad, that exists today; he should be interested in human cowardice or courage."

She also makes a very revealing statement about her attitude to criminals: "Criminals," she writes, "are dramatically interesting, because for a time at least they are active, free in spirit and they do not knuckle down to anyone . . . I think many suspense writers . . . must have some kind of sympathy and identification with criminals, or they would not become emotionally engrossed in books about them." A good writer, she goes on to state, has to look closely into the criminal mind and can only do so if he is sympathetic.

The first objective then, of a suspense novel is to create a feeling of menace and unease. This, you may argue, can also be central to a crime novel, and of course, at one level, this is so. However, the crime novel we have to remember, revolves round the solution of a crime, while the suspense novel on the other hand, relies on the evocation of a particular background from which a singular or series of singular situations emerge, where the outcome is not only in doubt but may also remain opaque. The reader knows that despite the apparent normality with which he is presented, deep and often sinister undercurrents shift uneasily beneath the bland surface.

The central core of the suspense novel lies in the gradual revelation of these undercurrents through the unmasking of characters and of situations. Given these objectives, it is not surprising that critics sometimes argue that a suspense novel is simply a work of fiction with suspense built into it.

Patricia Highsmith has dominated the field for nearly two decades but that is not to say that such writers as Margaret Millar, Celia Dale, Celia Fremlin, Ursula Curtiss and Margaret Yorke are not also outstanding practitioners of the art.

What are the techniques which all these writers use? On the whole their most successful novels (apart from Highsmith's *Ripley* series which are in a different class of their own) centre, as one would expect, on the ordinary and the mundane. A situation is described which, on the surface, appears familiar, rather dull. Gradually a mounting sense of frustration, of danger and of disintegration begins to make itself felt. A crime may or may not have been committed, but subtle hints that all is not as it seems inexorably lead the reader to mistrust the apparently placid tranquillity of the lives so carefully depicted by the writer. At the same time, the suspense lies as much in the motivation as in the untangling of complex personalities, in a growing apprehension that the characters' hold over events is fragile and insubstantial. In other words, the author has created a claustrophobic and irrational world.

Two interesting examples of Patricia Highsmith's art can be found in *The Sweet Sickness* and *People who knock on the door*. The former deals with a young man who, on the surface, appears to have everything; a brilliant academic record, a high salary and a girl who he plans to marry shortly, and for whom he has bought a beautiful house. He has one, apparently slight, problem in that his girl friend seems reluctant to make up her mind over the wedding date, but the hero, David Kelsey, doesn't see this as a major obstacle.

The reader is gradually made aware that Kelsey, who lives

in a boarding house, inhabits a fantasy world, and that his girl friend is already married and has no intention of changing husbands. The gradual deterioration of Kelsey's mind, his inability to come to terms with the real situation finally leads to murder and suicide. On the surface his life is exemplary, while his fellow lodgers see him as a shy, young batchelor in need of friends. To Kelsey however, they are simply a dull blur, at best inoffensive, at worst irritatingly intrusive. The hero's inner turmoil and disintegration is beautifully hinted at, but never outwardly discussed, so that the suspense and horror rely on a series of situations which gradually increase the tension as the book progresses.

This is the opening paragraph.

"It was jealousy that kept David from sleeping, drove him from a tousled bed out of the dark and silent boarding house to walk the streets."

Her aim here, Patricia Highsmith revealed, was to

"give a mood of emotional tension, of stubborn plodding, also, of a bottling up of force that will one day explode. If a person is so upset that he will get out of bed to take a lonely walk, he is in some kind of trouble."

Patricia Highsmith believes that writers should exploit particular plots which interest them, and that it is no bad thing to use them over and over again. Her most important theme, which she has used on many occasions is the 'relationship between two men, usually quite different in makeup, sometimes an obvious contrast in good and evil, sometimes merely ill-matched friends.' What this in turn achieves is surprise, the stretching of the reader's credulity, and above all that intimacy with the murderer himself.

Here is Kelsey, in his house in the country which he visits at weekends, and in which he makes believe he is visited by his girl friend Annabelle.

"At night, he slept with her in the double bed upstairs. Her head lay on his arm, and when he turned to her and held her close, the surge of his desire had more than once reached the summit and gone over with the imagined pressure of her body, though afterward, his hand, flat against the sheet, reported only emptiness and aloneness. On one Sunday morning, he threw away the bottle of Kashmir that he had bought because Annabelle had often worn it. He did not need such things to recall her. The perfume was even too much."

David Kelsey's relentless determination to make Annabelle marry him involves him in deceit, endless fantasy, and, unbeknown to her, the killing of her husband. Here he is, discussing his wedding plans:

"I realised I didn't answer one of your husband's questions and I didn't want him to think I was avoiding anything. The question was what's holding us up — Annabelle and me. She's had some trouble in her family you see. A death — or two. And I suppose that's what delayed us. Nothing more than that sir."
There was a terrible silence, and Dr Osbourne stared at him with his terrifying air of wisdom, and of disbelief."

In *People who knock on the door* Patricia Highsmith exposes the narrow minded malevolence, the intolerance and the hypocrisy of a small town caught up in the fervour of a religious revival, where self-righteousness ends in death, mental derangement and the disintegration of an ordinary family.

The technique here has certain similarities to *Sweet Sickness*. On the surface the family in question lead a normal suburban life. The suspense begins to unfold when the reader is gradually led to understand that the religious conversion of the father and the younger son makes them adopt attitudes which they believe to be normal but which the eldest son sees as cruel and vindictive. The tension between the two realities is finally brought to a climax by the shooting of the father by the young son who has discovered that the former, a fanatical denouncer of sins of the flesh, has made the local prostitute pregnant.

Celia Dale is another writer who skilfully reveals the nastiness beneath the apparently simple patina of every day life, producing stories with surprising twists at their end. A normal appearance will hide someone's strange secret, terror will slowly intrude into a straightforward situation. Domestic terror, in which she excels, is created drop by drop so imperceptibly that the full horror of the circumstances is only gradually accepted by the reader. Drab, bland lives conceal bizarre emotions and even more grotesque actions; small cruelties to helpless people unsettle and disturb. *A Helping Hand* provides a good example of her style.

The plot appears simple and understated. The Evanses like to give what they call 'a helping hand' to old ladies with nowhere to go. Through a chance meeting abroad old Mrs Fingal comes to live in their spare room and is subtly subjected to terror and exploitation; finally she dies. Behind the lace curtains of a small seaside resort lies anguish, clever deception and a cruelty which is delicately but frighteningly hinted at. A situation only half understood by the young Italian girl who comes to live with the Evanses for a time.

As they watch the television, the couple discuss future plans:

'In the living room Josh rubbed his hands. "Well that's good news, eh? An Italian cafe she said — fancy that."
   "I want her out of here before the summer."
   "But Mair, she'll be out of the house all day now."
   "I want her out of the house altogether."
   "You agreed she was useful. You agreed it looked well."
   "And so it did. But the point's been made. We want to keep to our timetable, don't we? With summer coming, the longer evenings, she'll be wanting to take the old lady out, get her mobile. She'll get her strength back. She'll even be offering to take her up to the Post Office and get her own pension, I shouldn't wonder . . .'
   "God helps those who help themselves. There's just one or two more things that girl will be useful for and then she's out. We can't keep Cynthia for ever."'

This kind of low key approach is also a characteristic of Margaret Yorke who portrays her characters in a careful and objective manner. As with Celia Dale and Patricia Highsmith the writing is controlled as the plot quietly unfolds. Ordinary people, leading unexciting lives, as in *The Hand of Death*, get caught up in murder and rape. The plot moves slowly and though the reader is aware of the identity of the murderer early on, the suspense is maintained throughout. Ordinary lives are closely observed from a different perspective. Here, the uncertainty lies as to how the criminal will behave. At the same time, as the main characters are fleshed out, the fears, the confusion and complexity of their lives, is gradually revealed, as is the effect that the crimes have on the quiet country town. It is a story about self-deception,

"I hope you weren't anxious, dear, when I was so late?"
"Oh no," said Nancy. "Why should I be? I knew it couldn't be anything serious."

And it is, of course, her husband who is both the murderer and the rapist.

In *The Smooth Face of Evil* we again have a story set quietly in a small country town where an elderly and lonely widow is befriended by a con man. On the surface a not particularly unusual situation, but as the novel slowly gathers pace, so the reader becomes aware of the grim cruelties of family life, of face saving gestures which hide both greed and a deep seated ambition. The pace is slow, but the suspense, implicit even in the first chapter, is beautifully hinted at and then gradually revealed as the first, petty, crime moves inexorably to a more serious one.

We have discussed Ruth Rendell's writing in a previous chapter, but no account of novels of suspense is complete without a mention of her work. She provides an interesting example of the difficulty of compartmenting the different genres of crime fiction. However, *A Demon in My View* provides an excellent model of a novel of suspense rather than crime. The first chapter sets the tone.

"He had never known how to talk to women. There was only one thing he had ever been able to do to women and, advancing now, smiling, he did it . . . Then he approached her, paralysed as she was, and meeting no resistance — he closed his hands on her throat . . .
He straightened her dress and replaced the handbag, which had come unhooked, once more on her arm. She was ready to die for him again."

Until she, a plastic model, is thrown out of the cellar, and Arthur Johnson has to find another neck to strangle.

Inevitable consequences follow. Here is the reader suddenly glimpsing the self-delusions under which Arthur lives, after his landlord has told him that a new tenant is about to move into the house.

"Good-looking young devil he is. Real flypaper for the girls, I shouldn't wonder."
Arthur couldn't bear that sort of talk. It made him feel sick. "I only hope he's got a good bank reference and a decent job."

The plot unwinds dramatically. After the doll is used as part of a Guy Fawkes bonfire, Arthur murders a woman who, it then turns out, lives in the same house, other tenants are revealed to lead secret lives, and finally he is unmasked by a surprising intervention.

Ruth Rendell's novels have all the ingredients of the classic work of suspense: she has a series of situations where the outcome is in doubt, suspense and not detection is the prime motivator; her characters are always complex, and the unrealised menace subtly portrayed.

Suspense novels evolve through characters rather than through the unwinding of an intricate plot. They explore the lives of victims who have no control over the events which have shaped their circumstances, and portray a world where things are never quite what they seem, and where not only an atmosphere of uneasiness prevails, but also a sense of menacing lurking forces silently manipulating a closed or isolated community.

Suggested reading:
Jessica Mann *Funeral Sites* (Macmillan)
Miles Tripp *High Heels* (Macmillan)
Celia Fremlin *The Parasite Person* (Gollancz)
Margaret Millar *Beast in View* (Gollancz)
Elizabeth Fenwick *Impeccable People* (Gollancz)
Margaret Yorke *No Medals for the Major* (Bles)

Chapter Five

The Private Eye

Are you hooked on the kind of pacy action usually found in stories with a private eye as the hero? Are you a secret fan of Philip Marlowe?

The history of the private eye detective novel stretches even further than that of the great classic whodunits. The first successful exponents of this genre were American writers, Dashiell Hammett, Raymond Chandler, followed later by Ross MacDonald, and now Robert B. Parker with his intellectual hero, Spenser. It is not so very surprising that this type of crime fiction has less appeal to British writers, though Dan Kavanagh, and on a different plane, Liza Cody, can be placed in the same category. American life, with its greater brutality, its very obvious corruption, its emphasis on the individualist ethic, has naturally provided a more suitable background to this genre. It is only recently, since the British have begun to take on board American values, that the world of the private eye has become more readily acceptable.

How do the Chandlers, the MacDonalds, the Parkers, develop their plots and produce their clues? With the private eye genre the plot is partly the action, and the clues are subsumed in the fast moving drama.

The momentum is achieved by the hero actively pursuing the clues while at the same time setting out to discover any person who might have even the most remote bearing on the situation. The plot therefore can often consist of a series of forceful interviews in which apparently little information is exchanged but which nevertheless produce a further momentum, and with it a new shift of perception. This series of vignettes provides a basic mechanism by which the plot building process is extended.

Clues are of course as necessary as they were in the works of the classical crime writers, but they are used in a different way. They often form part of the violence — the private eye looks round the scene of the crime, notices the manner in which the victim met his fate, may even comment on it, but because the action then speeds up that particular clue which has been presented to the reader will be lost in the ensuing scene. Two examples, the first from Dashiell Hammett, the second from Raymond Chandler, both brilliant practitioners of the throwaway clue, will show you what I mean.

"'Brains on her face,' he said. 'That seems to be the theme song of this case. Only this was done with just a pair of hands. But Jesus, what a pair of hands. Look at the neck bruises, the spacing of the finger marks.' 'You look at them,' I said. I turned away."

The finger marks are not referred to again, until we hear Marlow accuse Moose Molloy of having committed the murder. Molloy has previously been described as a man of vast girth, hence that particular clue, which is however immediately lost in the ensuing sudden flurry of activity.

The second example comes from *The Maltese Falcon*. Sam Spade has been asked to identify the body of his partner. He and the policeman who comes with him to look at the scene of the murder discuss the circumstances of the crime. The latter then says casually "That's it . . . The blast burnt his coat." And they continue to talk. The fact that there were powder burns on the coat meant that Archer must have allowed someone to approach him at close quarters — a friend and not an enemy. This provides the vital clue, which again is lost as the pace suddenly quickens.

What is also instructive in both examples is that the author makes the policeman and not the hero mention the clue; their statements are going to carry far less weight than if they had been made by the private eye.

It is interesting to trace the history of the genre. The originator was Dashiell Hammett, who with his *Continental Op* tales as well as his five crime novels, pushed the private eye novel out of the pulp magazine bracket and into a class of creative literature of its own. They are essential reading for any writer interested in producing this type of fiction. His successors owe much to the brilliance of his inventiveness, and to his imaginative probing of the reality of the world in which he found himself. His subtle unveiling of the complexities and ambiguities inherent in everyday situations form one of the main underlying themes present in most of his books. He produces a coherence and special vision which are instantly recognisable.

Hammett's formula rarely varies. The Op (or whichever private eye is the hero) finds himself in a situation where fantasy and lies are indistinguishable from each other. His reaction is to force the characters he meets to reveal yet more ambiguities, more violence, and more distortions of the truth. This in turn exposes yet more deceit and more dishonesty.

There are two other important elements in Hammett's work. The first is the belief that trust between people — whether they are part of the criminal fraternity or members of the apparently respectable outside world, is impossible. That being so, it is therefore irrelevant for whom the Continental Op, or Sam Spade, or whoever, work; they will always be surrounded by vicious and greedy phonies whose eye for the main chance is their most important motivation.

However, this cynical approach is linked to a second theme, strongly represented in most of the Hammett stories; the private eye is portrayed as very much a standard bearer, despite the world in which he moves, of incorruptability. This element is based both on a code of detection and the fact that Hammett's private eye always believes that his work is the most important part of his life. Here is Sam Spade:

"I'm a detective and expecting me to run criminals down and then let them go free is like asking a dog to catch a rabbit and let it go. It can be done, but it's not the natural thing."

Hammett's sharp laconic descriptions, as well as his neat

use of wisecracks, have continued to be seen as necessary components of any successful private eye novel.

"The pasty-faced informant was fairly bloated with pride in himself when he came through the door I had left unlocked for him. His swagger was almost a cake-walk; and the side of his mouth that twitches was twisted into a knowing leer that would have fit a Solomon."

Here is the Op reading a sign in a bar:

"Only genuine pre-war American whiskeys served here." I was trying to count how many lies could be found in those nine words, and had reached four, with promise of more, when one of my confederates, the Greek, cleared his throat with the noise of a gasoline engine's backfire."

If Dashiell Hammett created the first blue print for the private eye work of crime fiction, how have his successors added to the genre?

Most of those who followed in his footsteps accepted the guidelines but added their own interpretation. They have, on the whole, kept the hero as a man of action who forces the pace, a detective who sees the world from the outside, not because he feels he can play no part in society, but because he views it with a cynical, wry detachment.

How does the private eye differ from the detective portrayed in classical crime fiction? The most important difference is that the former sees himself as a professional actively engaged in seeking out the truth and in untangling the mystery; it is his job to do so. His predecessor, the amateur sleuth, on the other hand, thought nothing of arriving at a solution by a process of logical and relatively sedentary deduction. The private eye is the amateur on the move, the catalyst who creates a pace which, eventually, will in its turn produce the solution.

Pace, a certain detachment, as well as a sharp eye for detail, these are the crucial ingredients. Here are some opening paragraphs which encapsulate much of what I have described; the first comes from Raymond Chandler's *The Big Sleep*. His private eye is Philip Marlowe.

"It was about eleven o'clock in the morning, mid October, with the sun not shining and a look of hard wet rain in the clearness of the foothills. I was wearing my powder blue suit, tie and display handkerchief, black brogues, black wool socks with dark blue clocks on them. I was neat, clean, shaved and sober, and I didn't care who knew it. I was everything the well-dressed private detective ought to be. I was calling on four million dollars."

Chandler's use of short staccato phrases immediately creates the feeling of movement, while his tongue in cheek description of Marlowe's sartorial elegance is both sharp and witty.

Here is Ross MacDonald's private eye, Lew Archer, finding himself in much the same ambience — and reacting accordingly.

"I'd been hearing about the Tennis Club for years, but I'd never been inside of it. Its courts and bungalows, its swimming pools and cabanas and pavilions, were disposed around a cove of the Pacific a few miles south of the Los Angeles County border. Just parking my Ford in the asphalt lot beside the tennis courts made me feel like less of a drop-out from the affluent society."

MacDonald aimed, he once wrote, to make his detective the mind of the novel . . . 'a consciousness in which the meaning of other lives emerge.' The lives he portrays are lives of illusion, where people hide the truth about themselves from each other. Robert B. Parker, who is one of the latest to write in the Chandler tradition, has added a new ingredient to the formula with a hero who is very much the thinking man's private eye. This is not to say that the pace, the toughness and the wisecracks have been discarded, far from it; while his Spenser has much of the Hammett touch — a lonely Sir Galahad, and, appearances not withstanding, honourable and dedicated, in his fight against evil. Realism, a sharp dialogue, a moral message, these are some of the characteristics of Robert Parker's writing. His Spenser is a man of great moral sensitivity, with a wry sense of humour and a strong sense of good and evil.

The opening paragraph of *A Catskill Eagle* is a genuflection to both Hammett and Chandler.

"It was nearly midnight and I was just getting home from detecting. I had followed an embezzler around on a warm day in early summer trying to observe him spending his ill-gotten gain. The best I'd been able to do was watch him eating a veal cutlet sandwich in a sub shop in Danvers Square across from Security National Bank. It wasn't much, but it was as close as you could get to sin in Danvers."

The seediest private eye (and one of the most amusing) to come out of the British stable is Dan Kavanagh's ambidextrous hero Duffy. Though clearly less macho than his predecessors, he has the same ineffably cynical ability to distance himself from the action.

"There are too many ways of breaking a footballer's leg. Too many, that is, from the footballer's point of view. Others may find the freedom of choice encouraging."   *Putting in the Boot*

If pace is a vital ingredient how else, apart from moving the action along, do writers of private eye fiction achieve a momentum? If you read the books of any of the authors I have already mentioned, you will discover that the wise-cracking, which is found mostly in the dialogue, actually generates a pace of its own, as well as producing a feeling of events suddenly unfolding. The sharp raciness of the language keeps the reader particularly alert; its cynicism helps construct a unique picture of the private eye as an interesting anti-hero.

The private eye is a man who believes implicitly in the need to provide a solution to the problem in front of him, however painful this may turn out to be. It is this integrity, added to the way in which the reader is allowed into the hero's innermost thoughts, that builds up a portrait of a man fully committed to a cause.

Now let me give you two examples of the kind of dialogue I mentioned earlier. Note the economy of the writing. In the first Marlowe has been kidnapped by the opposition heavies.

"There was a little more silence, more curves, more winding ribbons of concrete, more darkness and more pain.
The Big Man said: 'Now that we are all between pals and no

ladies present we really don't give so much time to why you went back up there, but this Hemingway stuff is what really has me down.'

'A gag,' I said. 'An old, old gag.'

'Who is this Hemingway person at all?'

'A guy that keeps saying the same thing over and over until you begin to believe it must be good.'

'That must take a hell of a long time,' the big man said. 'For a private dick you certainly have a wandering kind of mind. Are you still wearing your own teeth?'

'Yeah, with a few plugs in them.'

'Well, you certainly have been lucky, pally.'"

What do we learn from the above dialogue? We see Philip Marlowe as an essentially lonely figure stoically surviving in an inimical and violent world. A man who manages to preserve his sense of humour irrespective of the perils of his situation. At the same time Chandler's underlying suggestion of menace produces both a sympathy in the reader and a wish to see how the situation will be resolved.

Robert B. Parker, in very much the same vein (some would even say with too much hint of pastiche) also moves briskly and economically through his dialogue.

"They weren't wearing guns, but each had a night stick in his hip pocket. The fat one took my arm above the elbow in what he must have felt was an iron grip.

'Start walking trooper,' he said, barely moving his lips.

I was frustrated and angry at Lowell Hayden, and at Mary Masculine, and the university. I said, 'Let go my arm or I'll put a dent in your face.'

'You and who else?' he said. It broke my tension.

'Snappy,' I said. 'On your days off could you come over and be my dialogue coach?'" *The Godwulf Manuscript*

If the private eye creates his own action in order to achieve a solution, this does not mean that the momentum makes him oblivious to those around him. Quite the contrary, he sees the world in sharp focus, the characters he comes across stand out clearly, their features and personalities drawn with a fine and observant pen. Descriptions tend to be memorable. Chandler again:

49

"He was a short thick man in a white coat. His eyes had a queer look, black and flat. There were bulbs of grey skin at the outer corners of them.

I turned my head on the hard pillow and yawned.

'Don't count that one Jack. It slipped out,' I said. He stood there scowling, his right hand hovering towards his right hip. Greenish malignant face and flat black eyes and grey white skin and nose that seemed just a shell." *Farewell My Lovely*

Ross MacDonald writes with the same clinical eye.

"I walked around to the front of the house and rapped on the screen door. Zinnie answered. She had changed to a black dress without ornament of any kind. Framed in the doorway, she looked like a posed portrait of a young widow, carefully painted in two dimensions. The third dimension was in her eyes, which had green fire in their depths." *The Doomsters*

There is a certain dichotomy in the role of the private eye. As we have seen, the reader is asked to view the detective as a lonely man honourably pursuing his search for the truth. I characterised the private eye as a kind of knight errant, the Sir Galahad of H. R. Keating's description. There is however little resemblance to Chaucer's 'gentle, parfitt' knight. The gentleness is hardly discernible as the hero, surrounded by the crooks and murderers of modern society, can only pursue his quest by violent action. The hero is realistically aware of the corruption around him and therefore believes that violence is the only way in which that corruption can be defeated. Sometimes, of course, violence is thrust upon him, at other times he sets out to produce specific scenes of disorder from which he knows he will emerge the victor.

Nevertheless, the private eye as a knight-errant and a man of integrity is a theme which runs through much of the literature. Here is Lew Archer, tempted to fill a junkie with drugs so as to make him talk.

"'Tell me what really happened.'

'Maybe I will, if you give me back my needle.'

His eyes held a curious mixture of plea and threat. They looked expectantly at the bright instrument in my fist. I was tempted to let him have it, on the chance that he knew something I could use. A few more capsules in those black veins wouldn't make any difference. Except to me.

I was sick of the whole business. I threw the needle into the square pink bath tub. It smashed to pieces." *The Doomsters*

The private eye as knight errant also feels a sympathy for the losers, the victims of shabby back street violence. Dan Kavanagh has neatly shuffled the ingredients to portray his hero as both a winner and a loser, a hero and a victim. This is Duffy, his sexually troubled hypochondriac.

"The second thing which had happened was that he had an erection. He didn't believe this either, but a check with the same fingertips confirmed the fact. *That*, Duffy, he said to himself, is a hard cock. Remember? The first one to come out of hiding for years. With Carol, that is.

There must be some explanation. Perhaps the two surprises were connected. Perhaps his cock was just a lymph node, and it was swollen now because he was going to die in a year or two of this terrible disease. But even so, that was definitely a hard cock.

Thank Christ Carol was asleep." *Putting in the Boot*

So far the examples I have used to show you the different ingredients which make up this type of genre have come from those novels whose heros are male and macho. Does this mean that it is difficult to have a woman private eye as a heroine? Liza Cody with Anna Lee and Sara Paretsky with W. I. Warshawski, to name but two, have proved otherwise. So women writers, do not be deterred! Liza Cody's heroine, unlike her male counterparts, works for a detective agency and not on her own. An acceptance of women's position in society? Perhaps. W. I. Warshawski, on the other hand, is her own boss.

How does Liza Cody put together the various necessary elements of private eye fiction? Firstly, she follows tradition in that she writes with a certain wry humour.

"You know, you really fascinate me. You have a hard sort of charm, and I never could resist bitchy girls. After all, you did send for me.'

Anna turned round. 'One,' she said sharply, 'I am not a girl. Two: I left a business card because I want to talk business. Three: if you haven't anything to say about Thea, piss off.'

'Well congratulations, you can count.' He got up and prowled over to the window, saying, 'You want something from me, and you ought to ask nicely.' He reached out and hooked his fingers in her belt. She kicked him smartly in the kneecap." *Dupe*

Cody also involves Anna in scenes of violence, even though she too, is portrayed as something of a loner, a woman anxious that others shouldn't be hurt.

"He got up to leave, suddenly embarrassed, and looking as out of place among the starched sheets as a dustbin in a ballroom.

'You are a bloody fool, though,' he said, hovering at the end of the bed. 'Why on earth didn't you scream or something? I'd have been up like a shot.'

'There wasn't time.' Anna closed her eyes. She didn't want to tell him that she hadn't yelled precisely because Bea or Selwyn would have come, and they might have been hurt too." *Dupe*

Sara Paretsky is sharper, tougher, given to more overt wisecracking — very much in the Chandler tradition. Karate expert and deadly marksman, Warszawski provides enough of her own violence and confusion to be taken seriously.

"He waved the gun at me and pointed down the stairs with his other arm. 'Beats me why well-paid hoods always dress so sloppily,' I commented. 'Your jacket doesn't fit, your shirt's untucked — you look like a mess. Now if you were a policeman, I could understand it . . ." *Indemnity Only*

And as for action:

"He was holding me too close, though I was able to turn slightly and bring my hand up with a short, strong chop, under his gun wrist. He let go of me but didn't drop the gun. I followed thro' with a half-turn that brought my right elbow under his armpit and made a wedge of my right fist and forearm. I drove into his ribs with my left hand, palm open, and heard a satisfying *pop* that told me I'd hit home between the fifth and sixth ribs and separated them." *Indemnity Only*

We have now discussed the major ingredients which make up a successful private eye story. Are there any pitfalls of which you should be aware before you start to tackle your own piece of writing?

Firstly, don't make your hero or heroine too violent, you will only produce a cardboard figure which is not what the reader is looking for. By all means make your private eye shabby, down trodden, even a victim, but don't allow him or her to be endlessly overtaken by events — your hero has finally to succeed. Even Duffy makes it, at whatever cost to himself. Remember, despite the wisecracks, this is a work of crime fiction, so do not rush to produce hilariously funny scenes, a cool cynical approach with a sharp dialogue is what is expected of you. Too much wisecracking can become pastiche — be warned! Robert B. Parker sometimes maintains an uneasy balance.

Don't provide action for action's sake. There is no point in your hero or heroine causing endless havoc for no purpose; each interrogation, each chase, must move the story logically along.

Finally, you must feel comfortable and believe in, the world you have created. Understand the ambitions and greed you describe, cast an objective eye on those your private detective meets, and remember that crime statistics are going up all over the world — there's plenty of room for a new private eye to emerge!

Suggested reading:
D. Kavanagh *Going to the Dogs* (Viking)
Raymond Chandler *Farewell My Lovely* (Hamish Hamilton)
Loren D. Estelman *The Midnight Man* (Hale)
Ross MacDonald *Blue City* (Cassell)

Chapter Six

Police Procedural

If you have always been fascinated by the nuts and bolts of criminal cases, then the police procedural is for you. The main thrust of this type of crime fiction deals with the way a police department reacts to the criminal cases with which it is presented. It is not, as we find in the worlds created by P. D. James or Ruth Rendell, a story which is viewed through the eyes of one policeman; that type of fiction, as we have seen, is a crime novel and not a police procedural.

So, what are the different elements which make up a police procedural? The main interest of the story, and one which differentiates it from other types of crime fiction, is the microscopic examination of the routine methodology of a police department faced with disentangling the effects of a serious crime, normally but not always, murder. The major part of the book therefore deals with the patient sifting of facts, routine questioning, the taking down of statements, an assessment of forensic reports, and so on. Clearly, some knowledge of how a police department works is essential, and is not as difficult to achieve as you might think. Most crime writers have found the police helpful, while senior police often give lectures to the Crime Writers Association, on various aspects of their work. Don't forget that policemen also write autobiographies from which much background can be gleaned, as it can from television and from other writers of the genre. The most important facet of police procedurals is that they show the police working as a team. It is therefore difficult, or can appear to be, to create a hero with whom the reader, as with the private eye, can empathise.

There are, however, ways round this. You can direct the limelight onto one particular policeman, describe some of the major characters so vividly that they all appear interesting and important or, by using the same police department in each story, highlight the different techniques used by the various teams of police officers.

Another crucial element of a police procedural is therefore to give your detectives a rounded personality, men and women whose private hopes and fears are as vital to the plot as is their teamwork.

The next problem to overcome is how to deal with the routine of a police investigation. Routine, by its very nature, is tedious. It is also the basis of all successful police inquiries. So — how do you make it interesting for the reader?

There are various ways of getting round this particular dilemma. The first is to describe the different elements of the case — how statements are obtained, how they are followed up, how alibis are checked out. By doing this you will have produced a three-dimensional description of the case.

Another method is to add pace and interest to the plot by having the team investigate a series of crimes rather than just one; this is how Dell Shannon and Lesley Egan solve the problem. In *Destiny of Death*, for instance, we find Shannon engaging the Luis Mendoza team in a stream of parallel crimes — a sudden spate of mugging, the imprisonment of a twelve-year-old girl by her foster mother, an elusive "Jack the Ripper" who achieves his getaway by going off with his victims' clothes, rapists on a university campus, and finally the murder of an invalid. All the crimes are investigated and all are solved. Four are described in the first twenty-six pages at the same time as the reader learns about the private lives of two of the detectives.

Ed McBain, in his 87th Precinct series uses the last three methods most effectively. And, if you are at all interested in writing police procedurals, you ought to see for yourself how he, the best and most accomplished writer in the field, deals with the problem of making teamwork appear both fascinating and true-to-life.

First, he has two groups of detectives who are seen as a

close-knit team but who are also portrayed as interesting and individual characters with their own problems, backgrounds, fantasies, and as such are instantly recognisable. Here is his description of one member of the 87th Precinct team, Meyer Meyer, a bald thirty-seven-year-old Jewish detective.

"He was, you see, a change-of-life baby. Now whereas news of an impending birth will generally fill the prospective parents with unrestrained glee, such was not the case when old Max Meyer discovered he was to be presented with an offspring. Max did not take kindly to the news. Not at all. He mulled it over, he stewed about it, he sulked, and finally he decided impulsively upon a means of revenge against the new baby. He named the boy Meyer Meyer, a splendid practical joke, to be sure, a gasser. It almost killed the kid." *King's Ransom*

This vignette, repeated in one form or another in all the 87th Precinct books makes it difficult for the reader ever to forget Meyer Meyer. And, at the same time McBain builds up the reader's knowledge of his characters by portraying them with their different problems (as, for instance, Bert Kling's love life) throughout the series.

Dell Shannon and Lesley Egan, two pen names used by Elizabeth Livingston, both as well known as Ed McBain, deal with the problem of the team by concentrating in some depth on the lives of its different members. Mendoza, Dell Shannon's captain in the Los Angeles Police Department, is of Spanish extraction, has inherited a fortune, and lives in a large house inhabited by small noisy twins, a red haired wife, a Scottish housekeeper, rare sheep, and talkative Siamese cats. Each of his colleagues' life style is also meticulously described so that the reader is constantly aware of the parallel lives of the police officers irrespective of what case they are investigating.

Another writer of the police procedural, Bill Knox, in his Colin Thane books, deals less with the routine and more with his Superintendent as leader of a team. Knox makes a particular point that even if the cases are different, the routine still stays the same — that despite this the writer can create a new situation simply by the way he describes the typing-up of reports, or the way in which a forensic laboratory works.

McBain again:

"Sam Grossman, an emotional man by nature, an unemotional man by trade, ran the lab with the uncompromising discipline of an African missionary. The lab, Grossman knew, would very often shorten the work of the men out there in the field. The lab could bring criminals to justice. And if he could help to do this, Grossman felt his life was not being wasted."

You could, of course, take a leaf out of McBain's books by adding as he does the drawings or photos of the evidence which are sent by the detectives to the police lab.

John Wainwright, one of the most prolific writers of the police procedural (himself an ex-policeman), uses the most boring routine of police work as a means of highlighting the complex emotions of his characters, both criminals and police. Two of his most minutely observed books, *All on a Summer's Day* and *All Through the Night*, simply but graphically show how policemen respond to the pressure of their job. Here he is describing a young policeman on the beat:

"It was very nice being on the street again. That's what bobbying was all about. Not sitting in an office all night answering telephone and teleprinter messages. That wasn't bobbying. THIS was bobbying.

"Higginbottom strolled along the parade of shops, checking each door as he passed. A sweet and steady number; official walking speed two-and-a-half miles per hour . . . that's what the book of words said and the book of words was always right." *All on a Summer's Day.*

A minute later he finds himself in a pork butcher's shop fighting off the advances of a St. Bernard.

And some chapters later the every day task of typing up reports is brought sharply into focus.

"every statement, every report, every everything. Six of 'em . . . and on a typewriter weak from rough usage. A man could go cross eyed in next to no time . . . He'd removed his coat and rolled up his sleeves, but the sweat dripped from his chin and his nose and, if he wasn't careful, stained, whatever it was he was wrestling with at the moment."

As the daily grind of a police department unfolds, and as the police set out to hunt murderers, thieves and petty criminals, Wainwright also allows us to have an insight into the private lives of his detectives. He uses the same approach in *All Through the Night*, a sequel to the earlier novel, but with a different setting and different characters.

However, in the latter book he relies far more on fast dialogue to produce its own momentum. The following extract shows one of the local policewomen interrogating a hardened young woman suspect. The dialogue not only moves the action along, but also allows the reader an insight into how Nash, the policewoman, approaches what is, after all, a very mundane interrogation.

"'You have to be joking!' Even Nash was shocked. 'You're asking for benzedrine? Amphetamine tablets? Do you realise where you are, young lady?'

'In the bleeding nick. Where else?'

'Well . . .' Nash swallowed. 'That's one thing that is *not* on the house.'

'Don't tell *me*' Fleming's curling lips made her mouth ugly.

'What?'

'You get 'em. Sodding hell . . . think we don't *know*? You get 'em, you take 'em. Everybody who can get the bleeding things takes 'em.'

Hold your water Fanny. Grab hold of yourself. This one is in a class of her own. She is a beaut and, when she nose-dives, she'll think the whole world has fallen on top of her. She needs *some sort of understanding. Work at it girl, work at it.*"

We are shown two other facets of police work — the way in which a young quasi-criminal presumes the police to be involved in shady schemes of their own, and as the obverse to this cynical approach, we see the police trying to arrive at some sort of understanding of the criminal mind.

The portrait of the policeman as a human being, caught up in problems of conscience or prejudice forms a strong element in the writing of J. J. Marric, one of the many pseudonyms of John Creasey, Marric's Commander Gideon series are not only excellent documentary novels about Scotland Yard, but also often mirror some of the social questions of the day. His hero Gideon is a beautifully rounded portrait of a man whose private life is seen as important as is his working day. Various investigations are carefully welded together, while the number of cases investigated add depth to Marric's portrayal of police team work, so that the result is a solid, always authentic, piece of writing.

In *Gideon's Art* for example, which on the surface appears to deal with the theft of some famous paintings, we not only find Gideon opening up the case of a man sent down for murdering his wife, but also becoming involved with the conscience of a racialist Superintendent in charge of an investigation into the smuggling of Pakistanis into the country.

"Above all, a policeman had to see a man *as* a man, not prejudge him because of colour or creed, nor even because he had a record as long as his arm. Such absolute objectivity was never easy . . . "Oh, to hell with it George! I can't stand them. I don't think they should ever have been allowed in. If I had my way I'd send them back bloody fast! . . . I saw one of the immigrants smuggled in three weeks ago. He lives in a hole under the stairs, there's no other word for it, rat-infested and filthy. It made me vomit when I saw it . . ."

"And where does that leave me?" demanded Riddell. "Right in the middle George. I can't think straight about it. I can't even think for myself over it, let alone think as a copper."

A different writer in this genre is Hilary Waugh whose Chief Fellowes series is more or less unique among police procedurals in that there is usually only one mystery to be solved, and that is as often as not accomplished more by the intelligent application of reason by the Chief than through team work. Both these writers are a must for those who wish to follow in this field.

The ingredients we have mentioned so far are pace, three dimensional characters, and the investigation of more than one crime. There is however one problem in discussing the daily routine of a police team's job, and that is that routine police work doesn't depend on brilliant deductive methods, but rather on the painstaking accumulation of statements and the slow sifting of evidence. Steady team work is the essence of police work. So if you faithfully imitate a real life situation you will inevitably produce a dull and plodding book. The way round this is to introduce some unexpected element — a strange crime, an original character, which adds both imagination and entertainment to your police procedural.

Ed McBain is a past master at appearing to deal with a genuine police department but at the same time producing bizarre cases for his 87th Precinct team to solve. Take three of his books — not necessarily his best, at random. In *King's Ransom* it is the chauffeur's son who is kidnapped not the son of the heir; in *Killer's Wedge* the widow of a criminal arrives at the precinct to kill the man who put away her husband, and threatens the detectives with a gun and a bottle of nitro-glycerine, and in *Let's Hear it for the Deaf Man* a man with a hearing aid presents endless clues to the men of the precinct, announces his intention to rob a bank, and finally succeeds in escaping capture. In that same book one of the detectives falls in love with the victim of a robbery and a policeman on the beat is found to be masterminding some local break-ins which have been baffling the detectives. All three stories have the same off beat and yet, perfectly realistic, quality.

Take the opening pages of *Killer's Wedge* which sets the scene.

"Like a well-constructed symphony, there was an immediately identifiable theme to the sounds inside the squad room. This theme was built on a three-part harmony of telephone rings, typewriter clackings and profanities. Upon this theme, the symphony was pyramided into its many variations. The variation ranged from the splendid *whooshy* sound of a bull's fist crashing into a thief's belly, to the shouted roar of a bull wanting to know where the hell his ball-point pen had gone, to the quietly persistent verbal bludgeoning of an interrogation session . . ."

Three pages later the peace is shattered and the routine broken.

"I'm waiting for Detective Carella," she said. "Detective Steve Carella," and she said the last words with surprising bitterness.

"If you're waiting for him," Hawes said patiently, "you'll have to wait on the bench outside. I'm sorry, but that's —"

"I'll wait right here," she said firmly, "And you'll wait too."

Hawes glanced at Meyer and Kling.

"Lady" Meyer started "we don't want to seem rude" . . .

"Shut up!" the woman said.

There was an unmistakable ring of command in her voice. The detectives stared at her.

Her hand slipped into the pocket on the right-hand side of her coat. When it emerged, it was holding something cold and hard.

"This is a .38," the woman said."

So what are the golden rules for police procedurals? Individual characters have to be clearly defined, there must be a good sense of locale, the established and formal machinery which is set in motion when a crime is discovered must be carefully exposed. If you think that you're going to write about a team of detectives in a series of books, then remember to vary the type of crimes you describe. Do what Ed McBain has done, and set your police station in a part of the world where all sorts of crime can be committed, and by different sorts, and classes, of people.

Suggested reading:
J. J. Marric *Gideon's Day* (Hodder & Stoughton)
Hillary Waugh *The Late Mrs D* (Gollancz)
Bill Knox *The Taste of Proof* (Longman)
James McClure *The Sunday Hangman* (Macmillan)

Chapter Seven

The Thriller

For the sake of clarity I have decided to divide the thriller into two categories; the first I shall call the action thriller, the second the espionage novel. I will deal with the latter in the next chapter. The difference is relatively clear cut. In the spy novel the heroes always have links with the world of intelligence, of which they are, however tenuously, a part. In the former, perhaps best exemplified in the works of Dick Francis, the purpose of the book is to produce a work of fast action. Criminals, rather than spies, are the villains of the piece.

If you feel that you're most interested in fast action, don't want to involve yourself in the specifics of the private eye or the spy novel, then this genre might suit you best. It may also be for you if you have a specialised knowledge of particular subjects, know about the computer industry, about oil rigs, motor car racing.

So what constitutes a thriller? Of course, many of the ingredients we have come across in other forms of crime fiction apply to this type of writing. Pace is of the utmost essence — something has to happen on every page, and usually to the hero. The bad guys are straightforward criminals, not as in the spy novel, the arm of the enemy state.

The latest generation of writers of the genre have produced what might best be called the 'big bang' action thriller. Frederick Forsyth and Ken Follett are two most famous examples of this type of crime fiction. Both are journalists, both rely heavily on research, and both reveal the dangers inherent in modern technology. Forsyth specialises in 'documentary' stories, Follett pursues the possibilities which lie behind specific historical events.

So, if you want to follow in the footsteps of Ken Follett, or Frederick Forsyth, your most important ingredient must be pace. Something must happen or be about to happen on every page. The tension must evolve from the pace, the hero or heroine have to find themselves in situations which in themselves create immediate and sudden responses. The characters and the theme have to be sharply defined — good versus evil, the welfare of the state versus the ambitions of the individual. The dialogue must be terse; famous events hinted at in the background. The interest can be sustained by the use of characters with different objectives, different allegiances and different ambitions. The end needs to be ingenious but thoroughly satisfying.

How did the early thriller writers approach their subject? If we examine the work of John Buchan, master craftsman, we find, as say, in *The Thirty Nine Steps*, that his criminals could also be spies. Even now however, despite its racist and blinkered view, the book provides the reader with a carefully crafted example of how thrillers should evolve. It has a clever mixture of surprising situations, a thrilling chase across the country from the north of Scotland to southern England, and a number of enemy aliens. A classic of its kind.

The most famous of the modern thriller writers is undoubtedly Dick Francis. What is the secret of his success?

Francis writes to a certain formula based on three main ingredients. In the first place his writing is simple and uncluttered. Because his sentences are short this produces a feeling both of pace and tension. Second, he creates his heroes as sympathetic characters with whom the reader — whether he knows anything about horse racing or not, can easily identify. His criminals on the other hand, are revealed as deeply flawed and evil human beings. Francis quite clearly sets out to paint a distinctly black and white picture of his characters, while at the same time making the reader subtly aware of his compassionate and humane view of society. His plots are carefully constructed, in that whatever the twists and turns, the outcome emerges as a natural part of the story. The logic of the plot produces that gripping tension for which the writer is so justly famous, as of course does the inevitable chase which is central to the book. The author's opening paragraphs usually provide a glimpse of the coming action.

Below are two examples, one written in 1964, the other some 19 years later.

"Art Mathews shot himself, loudly and messily, in the centre of the parade ring at Dunstable races.

I was standing only 6 feet away from him, but he did it so quickly that had it been only 6 inches I would not have had time to stop him." *Nerve*

"There was a God-awful cock-up in Bologna. I stood as still as possible while waves of cold rage and fiery anxiety jerked at my limbs and would have had me pacing.

Stood still . . . while a life which might depend on me was recklessly risked by others. Stood still among the ruins of a success nearly achieved, a freedom nearly won, safety within grasp." *The Danger*

The same short sentences and the same atmosphere of drama and tension immediately engage the reader's attention.

The Francis hero also follows a set pattern. He is dependable, slightly awkward, always honest and very often lacks self-confidence. This mixture produces immensely likeable characters to whom the reader has no difficulty in relating partly because they are relatively ordinary, even though, at another level, somehow unique.

The dialogue is spare and laconic, often highlighting the hero's attractive, self-deprecating character.

The following passage is a good example of the Francis formula.

"She rides, you know," she said as Bob led the watered horse off to an empty box, "but only up on the Downs. She goes up and down with me in the Land Rover. We don't discuss it. It's routine."

"How is she otherwise?"

"Much happier I'd say." She grinned hugely and clapped me lightly on the shoulder. "Don't know how anyone so cold can bring someone to life."

64

"I'm not cold," I protested.

"No?" She considered me quizzically. "There's a feeling of iron about you. You're not intimidating . . . but I'm sure you could be if you tried." *The Danger*

The hero not only has an attractive personality but he is also courageous. Like James Bond he has great powers of perseverance which enable him to think through and overcome situations of violence and danger.

"Desperation can move mountains. I'd never hoped to have another minute alone to put it to the test, but I'd thought of a way of detaching myself from the man's box, if I had enough strength. Yardman had had difficulty squeezing the rope down between the banding bar and the wooden box side when he'd tied me there: he'd had to push it through with the blade of his penknife. It wouldn't have gone through at all I thought, if either the box side wasn't a fraction warped or the bar a shade bent. Most of the bars lay flat and tight along the boxes, with no space at all between them.

I was standing less than 2 feet from the corner of the box: and along at the corner the bar was fastened by a lynch pin." *Flying Finish*

If the obstacles are spectacularly outmanoeuvred, the crimes themselves are never ordinary, but often so outrageous and unacceptable that the reader is totally alienated from those who commit them. Dick Francis has created a convention which is very much his own, of the hero who is, despite his unwillingness, reluctantly pushed into situations which lead to destruction and aggression. This approach distinguishes the Francis type of crime fiction from the spy thriller where (as in Adam Hall's Quiller series) the reader is willing to accept that the spy may well initiate a chain of events which ultimately ends in violence; the rationale behind this apparent pursuit of aggression being that the spy is seen as defending his country against those who conspire against it.

In the thriller the aggression is acceptable because the hero fights for his life. This moral justification, which is seen as permitting acts of violence, is central to such authors as

Buchan, Desmond Bagley, Alistair MacLean, Ken Follett, whose heroes pit their wits successfully against difficult climactic and human odds.

Alistair MacLean and Desmond Bagley encapsulate the spirit of the 1960s; Ken Follett and Duncan Kyle represent the next two generations of thriller writers. The work of the former is very much that of the adventure thriller, packed with action, much of it with the hero facing bitterly adverse weather conditions, while at the same time pursuing or being pursued by the enemy. Maclean, for instance, specialises in ice blizzards and generally frightening natural disasters which add a secondary tension to the chase itself. As the plot moves briskly from one horrifying episode to the next so the end is satisfyingly simple.

MacLean has written not only adventure stories but also thrillers such as *Puppet on a Chain* where the hero sets out on a personal crusade – in this case to discover and defeat the enemy, a group of men who are masterminding a famous drug ring. Though the book is flawed, it repays a close analysis, in that the writing, the plot, the characterisation, as well as the dialogue, reveal why it is that MacLean has always maintained his place at the top of the best seller list. It also highlights one of his major weaknesses; the cardboard character of his female personalities. In *Puppet on a Chain* the hero, a major in Interpol's Narcotic Bureau, arrives in Holland with two female agents who are to provide his backup. One is a beautiful brunette, the other a curvaceous blonde, the description of whose clothes, dialogue and feelings produces unnaturally wooden characters who add little to the plot. So make yourself a note — if you don't feel too happy with women characters, then try to introduce them as little as possible!

If MacLean's women are cardboard, the criminals are also stereotyped — but their malevolence is such that the reader finds them acceptable. The dreadful Reverend Goodbody, oozing apparent sweetness and light while at the same time shown to be a mad, demonic villain; the unlikely Morgenstern and Muggenthaler, hugely obese and deeply sinister; and even the corrupt policeman who turns out to be the master mind behind the drugs syndicate, all, in their grotesqueness, engage the imagination of the most susceptible of readers.

So, given these major flaws, how does MacLean persuade the reader to turn the page? He does so in different ways — not only does something happen in every chapter, but the events are so bizarre that the reader has to hurry on in order to discover how the hero can possibly extricate himself from the latest disaster which has befallen him. There is no time to think, only to marvel. MacLean's other trick, and here he joins company with Dick Francis, is to portray the hero so sympathetically that the reader will happily identify with him. He will be seen as a man who is generous and honourable, a crusader pitted against the evil doers who are the enemies of society, and therefore whose aggression and even cruelty can be forgiven. Every chapter is 'action packed'. The book starts off with the murder of a man who was to have produced vital inside information on the drug trade. This is immediately followed by a chase, a climb over rooftops, another death, the discovery of a secret code, a meeting with the head of Amsterdam police, a sighting of four murdered bodies and the introduction of Trudi, the apparently drug addicted daughter of a senior police official. All within the space of the first fifty pages! As each new character is introduced, each in turn produces novel and unlikely situations.

And as the pace moves the reader relentlessly forward, so the atmosphere of a murky grey, secretive and rain sodden city is deftly presented. The following extract gives the reader the initial description of the warehouse which later figures prominently in the plot.

"I stopped at a corner and watched him make his way along a narrow, ill-lit and singularly unlovely street, lined exclusively by warehouses on both sides, tall five-storey buildings whose gable roofs leaned out towards those on the other side of the street, lending an air of claustrophobic menace, of dark foreboding and brooding watchfulness which I didn't much care for at all."

MacLean relies not only on pace but also on the bizarre and the outrageous. Puppets which move of their own volition, churches as centres of the drug trade, addicts dressed up as nuns, life size puppets, and later dead victims hung on chains outside warehouses, night club owners locked up in their own wall safes, each situation keeps the reader moving breathlessly forward, as the hero narrowly escapes death, is caught again and finally triumphs over evil.

The penultimate crisis, which is particularly horrifying, illustrates Maclean's versatility. The hero discovers, as he is chained to the wall, that the enemy plan to make him insane by bursting his ear drums with the noise of amplified clock chimes.

"He clamped the sorbo-rubber ear phones to my head and secured them immovably in position . . . Momentarily the room became almost hushed — the earphones were acting as temporary sound insulators. Goodbody crossed the room towards the amplifier, smiled at me again and pulled a switch. I felt as if I had been subjected to some violent physical blow or a severe electrical shock . . . My ears, my entire head, were filled with this insanely shrieking banshee cacophany of sound. It sliced through my head like white-hot skewers, it seemed to be tearing my brain apart."

This is only matched by a fight to the death which takes place on top of a huge crane which hangs over Amsterdam's dock yards. The hero kills the villain in an astonishing act of courage and is finally rewarded by the love of the curvaceous blonde. The reader can breathe a sigh of relief.

What is the basis of the Follett formula? There is a world of difference between his approach and that of Maclean. The latter, as we have seen, relies on a central figure through whose eyes the action is perceived. Follett, on the other hand, uses a more varied approach — the events are seen through the eyes of two or three protagonists who are given the same level of importance in the plot. His book *Triple* for instance, follows two main characters in a fast moving plot based on Israel's need to obtain enough uranium to enable her to manufacture her own atomic bombs. His parallel plot consists of the search for each other of these two characters, one a Russian communist, the other a member of Mossad, the Israeli secret service. Follett constantly changes the tempo of the writing, moves the action briskly across different parts of the world, introduces a love element, and has an excellent ear for dialogue. Because the events are viewed from a double perspective, the reader feels at the centre of every action — a highly successful method of communication. We follow the Israeli intelligence officer, his convoluted and highly secret journey to find, and then steal, the uranium, while at the same time we know that his opposite number in Moscow has discovered the purpose of his apparently unpremeditated travels, and is determined to stop him.

Part of Follett's formula is also to involve the reader and persuade him of the credibility of his main characters and their ability to discuss affairs with world famous figures; the titillation of inside knowledge.

"A moment later Rostov heard the deep confident voice of Yuri Andropov, one of the most powerful men in the world. "You certainly managed to panic young Edvardovitch, David."

"I had no alternative, sir."

"All right, let's have it. It had better be good."

"The Mossad are after uranium."

"Good God."

"I think The Pirate is in England. He may contact his embassy. I want surveillance on the Israelis there, but an old fool called Petrov in London is giving me the runaround."

"I'll talk to him now, before I go back to bed."

"Thank you sir."

"And David?"

"Yes?"

"It was worth waking me up — but only just."

Follett also accepts the mores of the spy novel, in that his heroes believe that their actions are morally justified if they are committed in defence of the state, though to make his partiality clear to the reader Rostov, the Russian intelligence officer, is shown to be more motivated by personal ambition than love of country. Here Follett's *Triple* bears a strong resemblance to the novels of Dick Francis, in that his Israeli is portrayed as a sensitive and sympathetic figure.

"Nat Dickstein was afraid.

He had never come to see himself the way others did, as a competent, indeed brilliant, agent who had proved his ability to survive just about anything. Later, when the game was on and he was living by his wits, grappling at close quarters with strategy and problems and personalities, there would be no room in his mind for fear; but now, when Borg was about to brief him, he had no plans to make, no forecasts to refine, no characters to assess. He knew only that he had to turn his back on peace and simple hard work, the land and the sunshine and caring for growing things . . ."

Here, the underlying assumption is that the hero is a gentle unassuming man who is, for the greater good of his country, forced into a life of violence, pain and death.

The difference of approach to Rostov is quite pronounced, as the reader is subconsciously asked to compare the two.

"The file made it clear that Dickstein was now one of the most formidable agents in the Mossad. If Rostov could bring home his head on a platter, the future would be assured.

But Rostov was a careful operator. When he was able to pick his target, he picked easy ones. He was no death-or-glory man: quite the reverse. One of his most important talents was the ability to become invisible when chancy assignments were being handed out. A contest between himself and Dickstein would be uncomfortably even."

As you can see, the thriller, despite the possibility of wide ranging subject matter, also has certain characteristics which need to be kept in mind if you are to achieve a successful outcome.

Suggested reading:
Gavin Lyall *Judas Country* (Hodder & Stoughton)
Nicholas Luard *Travelling Horseman* (Weidenfeld & Nicolson)
Desmond Bagley *The Vivero Letter* (Collins)
David Brierley *Checkmate* (Collins)
Eric Ambler *A Kind of Anger* (Bodley Head)
Harry Patterson *Comes the Dark Stranger* (Long)

Chapter Eight

The Espionage Novel

In the last chapter I pointed out that there was a good deal of difference between that type of crime fiction which deals with fast moving action where 'the enemy' might or might not be a foreign agent, and books which are wholly involved with the world of intelligence.

The spy novel is essentially about deviousness, about honour and dishonour, about treachery, and about the twilight world of the half truth. It is these characteristics which set it apart from other crime fiction.

The most famous spy novelists, (essential reading for the would be practitioner of the art form) are John Le Carré, Len Deighton, Charles McGarry, Ted Allbeury and Brian Freemantle. What exactly is it that differentiates them from other crime fiction writers?

Novels about espionage are primarily based on the premise that the reader need not necessarily know how the hero, or, as is sometimes the case, the anti-hero, discovers the truth about the opposition. The reader is expected to approve major convolutions of plot, distortions and hidden depths in characters, as well as to accept that nothing is as it seems. The effect of these parameters is to enhance the figure of the hero, who may well remain an opaque creation. At the same time the dialogue, as opposed to any other book of crime fiction, may well, legitimately, have an obliqueness which would not be permitted in any other example of the genre. Double meaning is here perfectly acceptable and is seen as adding to the atmosphere.

The introductory description of George Smiley in *Smiley's*

People encapsulates the flavour so particular to novels of espionage.

"He sat without expectation. He sat like an old man at a country railway station, watching the express go by. But watching all the same. And remembering old journeys."

Here is Smiley, seen not only as a self-effacing ancient spy catcher, but one who also, so the reader is made to feel, has hidden depths and memories which will eventually be revealed. And that is exactly what happens. The layers are gradually peeled back, but with such subtlety, such obliqueness, that any certainty as to the truth of certain events is always left in doubt. The story moves from London to Paris, to Moscow, Switzerland and back to London again; plots and subplots are revealed, only to be discarded as ephemeral, extra diversions from the real but hidden meaning which will finally emerge.

So here we have two of the main ingredients of the spy novel; the unglamorous shadowy figure of the spy, and a plot based on intricate dealing and double dealing.

These two characteristics are to be found not only in Le Carré but also in the work of the other outstanding writers working in this genre. Len Deighton is a past master of the obfusc and of the spy as the anti-hero. In his first successful novel, *The Ipcress File*, his hero is a grey, seedy and somewhat insalubrious character of doubtful antecedents, while his latest trilogy, *Game Set and Match*, shows him weaving an intricate and highly convoluted plot round a shady intelligence officer this time with suspect ambitions. Central to Deighton's plot is a third ingredient, also a major component of any work of spy fiction, the unmasking of the mole hidden at the centre of a particular intelligence network.

The plot within a plot within a plot (not for nothing do covers of spy novels show Russian dolls on the frontispiece) is usually achieved through some deception surrounding the central character. Anthony Price, on the other hand, whose hero Audley heads a shadowy government department, employs a different mechanism; he uses the past in order to enlighten the present. In one of his most carefully constructed plots, *Tomorrow's Ghosts*, he has one member of an intelligence team investigating the past of her superior. This device allows the author to produce elusive assassins, possible moles, and a considerable amount of shady double-dealing. The hint of murky deception is neatly suggested in the opening sentence:

"After only a week of exposure to her, Gary the Messenger Boy was ready to die for Marilyn the Temporary Secretary, Francis judged. So it was his good fortune that the scenario did not envisage his role as being self-sacrificial." *Tomorrow's Ghost*

The most extravagant example of the shady anti-hero is Brian Freemantle's intelligence agent, Charlie Muffin. More often a loser than a winner Charlie (though eventually always a survivor) not only fights his opponents but also has a running battle with his establishment colleagues whom he dislikes and who in turn try to finish him off. The following description highlights his unglamorous persona:

"Charlie Muffin wedged the saturated suede boots beneath the radiator, then spread his socks over the metal ribs to dry. There was a faint hiss of sound.
The bottom of his trousers, where the rain coat had ended were concertinaed and sodden and he felt cold, knowing his shirt was wet where the coat had leaked." *The Inscrutable Charlie Muffin*

The spy novel is more of a British invention than an American. Whether this is chance or, as some have claimed, is due to the devious and hypocritical nature of the British character is difficult to judge. There is no doubt that the British are obsessed by secrecy. And it is also true that British interest in spying has been kindled by the defection of such spies as Philby and Maclean and the unmasking of Anthony Blunt. It may simply be that Americans like their plots pacy rather than convoluted, so that it is only recently that they too have become interested in the spy genre.

There is one American writer however, Charles McCarry, who has for some time written of the American intelligence world very much as has Le Carré of the British. His central character is a poet, an intelligence officer called Paul Christopher.

McCarry uses the same devices — the search in the past for hidden secrets, a solitary spy leading a strange and difficult double life:

"Christopher went everywhere in the world, looking for men who were capable of acting, and making it possible for them to act . . . he worked with his mind and his personality: he formed secret friendships. Bribery, coercion, threats were no use to him; he wanted agents whom he could liberate, through his expertise and his government's money, to be themselves. He was alone, a singleton in the jargon, living under deep cover, with an ordinary passport and no protection from his government." *The Secret Lovers*

Another ingredient of the spy novel, and one which again sets it apart from other crime fiction, is the way that language is used. This can be seen at two different levels. The first is the use made of specialised jargon; the second is the way both dialogue and narrative are often presented in an opaque manner. Below is an example of the first:

"They used word code, he tells me. Old pals, they know how to fox around. But not with the proof, says Vladi, with the proof there's no foxing at all. No phones, no mails, no trucks, they got to have a camel, period. Vladi's security-crazy, okay, this we know already. From now on, only Moscow Rules apply." *Smiley's People*

This mannered approach enables the reader to enter into a special secret world, and makes that world more interesting and enticing because it is seen as unique. The use of jargon persuades the reader he has been allowed to participate in a mysterious and menacing private universe with its own code of behaviour and rationale, but one which will eventually yield up its secrets.

"All that remains, I guess, is to spring the news on Cerrutti," Patchen said.
    "And wait for the mousetrap to spring."
    "Your mouse, Paul, and your trap. You're looking a little haggard. It's a costly business, curiosity." *The Secret Lovers*

So we have the gradual unravelling of the different layers of the plot made more mysterious by the secret language that is used. This makes pace a less essential ingredient than in the action thriller though happenings need to occur if only further to muddy the waters. The world of intelligence has to be perceived as both subtle and fearful.

Bryan Forbes encapsulates that dichotomy in his *The Endless Game*

"He was protecting whoever protected him. A maze within a maze Alec. But you chose to ignore my advice. That's the impulsive streak in you. It's held you back, Alec, denied you the promotion your talents deserve. Our lords and masters feel uneasy with individuality. They like the status quo, the comforting warmth of what was shall always be, forever and ever, amen. I sometimes think they will us to stumble and fail; its something that gives them more power over us. They can never quite come to terms with the fact that we are a secret organisation. They like to hold all the secrets in their own hand."

Let us turn to one of the most important elements of the espionage novel, the unmasking of the mole or double agent. This is often used in conjunction with another, as serious, revelation, that is, the exposure of a major plot either against the state or the intelligence community. Previously this has been seen to be the work of the KGB, but nowadays the blame has also begun to fall on the CIA, and in some cases on secret departments of British intelligence.

One characteristic which links the spy novel to the modern crime novel is the importance given to the description of characters. In the latter, as we have seen, the character of the detective, as well as sometimes, that of the victim and the murderer, is central to the plot. The why-dun-it is as important as the who-dun-it. The spy novel also relies heavily on the gradual unfolding of the personalities of the main characters, but there is less interest in the reasons why a particular crime should have been committed, and more in why someone could become a traitor. This question of treason often leads to an exploration of questions of honour and dishonour, of the delicate balance between treason and valour. As one of Charles McGarry's characters says:

"It's not fully appreciated outside our little profession that it's sometimes an honourable act to commit treason." *The Secret Lovers*

Another theme, which Graham Greene explored so brilliantly in his *The Human Factor* was that of gratitude and betrayal, the one leading to the other. Here is the hero's mother reminiscing on his early childhood:

"You always had an exaggerated sense of gratitude for the least kindness. It was a sort of insecurity, though why you should have felt insecure with me and your father . . . You once gave away a good fountain-pen to someone at school who had offered you a bun with a piece of chocolate inside it."

Castle, the son, sees himself differently:

"Everything would be looked after for better or worse by somebody else. Somebody with the highest professional qualification. That was the way death ought to come in the end, he thought, as he moved slowly and happily in the wake of the stranger. He always hoped that he would move towards death with the same sense that before long he would be released from anxiety for ever."

We now come to a different type of spy novel, one which, as I previously mentioned, is an extension of the thriller — the action spy thriller. This type of crime fiction while it still deals with the grey and twilight world of intelligence differs from it in four different ways. First it relies on pace as one of its main ingredients. The reader may still have to unravel the convolutions of a many layered plot, but the speed of the action is the main motor which propels the book along.

The second difference lies in the presentation of the agent as a man of daring and machismo. In the more traditional spy story the hero is shown as an amorphous murky creature who slips easily into the background, one who, despite the major role he plays in unmasking the traitor, is not seen as a man of action. The hero of the fast espionage thriller, 007 and Adam Hall's Quiller for example, is central to the action. The effect of the change of roles is to magnify the hero and to diminish and simplify the plot. No longer is the process of intellectual and patient reconstruction of such a one as Smiley a major element of the book.

The third and fourth different ingredients, though not necessarily always included in all spy thrillers, are the importance sex and overt violence play in the plot. Ian Fleming used both in his books. Adam Hall in his Quiller series includes only the latter.

How does Ian Fleming, the man who more than any other writer created the post war action packed spy novel, produce the unique mixture of pace and the world of intelligence, which made him so famous?

Fleming in creating his 007 created a myth. He did this partly because James Bond could be accepted (he was of course writing at the height of the cold war) as a knight errant pitted against the forces of evil, and partly because Bond represented the public face of the new affluence of the post war era. 007 appeared to encapsulate in a romantic fashion that extraordinary era of 'never had it so good.' Elegance, charm, pace and the smiting of the overmighty enemy (a nostalgic return in a sense to the old fairy tales of a past age of good and overcoming evil), were the ingredients which made 007 the darling of millions. In the first twenty six pages of *Casino Royale* (first published in 1953) James Bond wins three million francs at the gaming tables, watches a Russian agent try to out-gamble him, is sent by his boss to defeat agents of SMERSH the most fanatical department of the NKVD, and has his room bugged and his operation blown wide open. At the same time he learns that his assistant on the job is to be a beautiful girl. And now read on!

Adam Hall has a different technique. His secret agent, Quiller, is usually sent in to places where violence is about to erupt because, like 007, he is considered to be a man who gets results. The personality of the hero, and the nature of the action carries the plot. Hall achieves his pace in two different ways. First, like Fleming, as much as possible happens in as short a time as possible. If we look at the first twenty six pages of his *The Striker Portfolio*, the hero finds himself in West Germany watching planes fall out of the sky; returns to London to be obliquely briefed by his control; flies to Amsterdam, on to Hanover, finally to discover that his arrival causes the opposition to murder the man who was to be his informant.

The second method that Adam Hall uses which is particular to himself, is to have a strangely violent yet obscure language which by its obliqueness reminds one of some of Le Carré conversations, but which in fact add to the pace.

"I walked for a bit and he didn't break the silence. I don't like being used as a hooded falcon. I couldn't do anything about it, of course. You're cleared, briefed and sent in and if you ask any questions outside the prescribed limits of the briefing they think you're nosey or windy and they're usually right."

Here are the opening paragraphs of *The Warsaw Document*.

"There would be no warning, I knew that.

In the total darkness I thought I could see things: the glint of his eyes, his bared teeth; and in the silence I thought I could hear his breath and the soft tentative padding of his feet as he looked for me; but all I saw and heard was in my imagination and I knew that soon my nerves were going to start playing up because of the worry: the worry that there'd be no warning when he came at me. He'd come the instant he found me."

Here again is the macho spy, the man of action rather than the man of intellect; a man who combines pace with violence. Different to Bond, Quiller's sexual preferences are only hinted at, perhaps a possible romance, but tantalisingly nothing more. The macho image and the pace are built up by the use of short staccato sentences which hurry the reader inexorably on to the next page, and the next act of violence. The dialogue has a set pattern:

"No go," I said.
   "That's what I told him."
   "I work best alone, you know that."
   "That's what I told him."
He'd been enjoying himself, telling Parkis the answers before I'd been given the questions.

78

"All I haven't told him," he said carefully "is whether you've dug up any lead-in data at Linsdorf."

"I've been down there for twelve hours, remember?"

"That's all right. I just asked. Because he will. How's the hand?"

"Top condition."

"And what else was it? The arm, wasn't it?"

"I still don't want a shield."   *The Striker Portfolio*

So there we have it. Two types of espionage novel. The first we might call the intellectual's, the second the man of action's. Introspection is a major feature of the former, pace and violence of the latter. At the heart lie the same kind of questions — matters of honour, of treason and of betrayal. Elliptical descriptions are also often married to a convincingly detailed portrayal of the world of espionage where the spy is seen as a civil servant, some kind of faceless bureaucrat whose world is made up of deceptions and trickery. It is an enclosed world unique in its isolation where action is rarely related to outside pressures, but where its internal codes become a way of life. That isolation is reflected in language, in objectives, and in a blinkered approach towards specified and unspecified goals.

Suggested reading:
Ted Allbeury *Consequence of Fear* (Collins)
Bryan Forbes *The Endless Game* (Collins)
Charles McCarry *The Miernik Dossier* (Hutchinson)
Len Deighton *Funeral in Berlin* (Cape)
John Le Carré *The Honourable Schoolboy* (Hodder & Stoughton)

Chapter Nine

How Some Authors Write

I thought it might be interesting and useful for you if I asked some practitioners of the art how they wrote their books. By so doing you could gain something from their experience. So I decided to interview four authors, each of whom has written books in a different genre to that of the others. The writers I spoke to were Jessica Mann, Peter Dickinson, Colin Dexter and Anthony Price. They represent the suspense novel, the crime novel, the detective novel and the intellectual man's espionage novel.

Why did I choose these authors? Because, even though they may not be as famous as some, I believe they are among the best of those writing in their particular genre. You may not agree, but for me all four writers have something rather special to them, a spark which sets them apart, an approach to their work which is always interesting. Let me describe some aspects of their work so that you can understand why I chose them. To begin with I think that what is central to all four is their intelligent use of language and the care of their prose style, an attribute often missing in the work of crime fiction writers. Clearly they are writers who think carefully about the craft of writing.

The effect of this is to produce clarity and precision, even though they might, as in the case of Anthony Price, often choose to be elliptical. It is also apparent that they are interested and curious in the way people react to events; it is their characters, often slightly off beat, who form the central interest of their books. Events crowd round them but do not obtrude.

All four have a wonderful sense of history, perhaps not

surprising given their interest in military history, archaeology, African history and, with Colin Dexter, a delight in the historic past of Oxford.

Jessica Mann's writing has been characterised as possessing a literacy, a sense of unease that sinister things are happening behind closed doors, and a sense of place, which makes the reader feel that he is returning to a much loved country. She manages successfully to create whole communities, conveying their individual personalities in a prose that one reviewer has called, 'clean, correct and un-frilly.' Her writing is always assured and stylish, while at the same time understated, so that the pervasive menace and obscure ambiguities which are part of the strength of her work are achieved by oblique inference, through small details and observations.

I asked Jessica Mann why she wrote crime fiction and not straight novels? A question which perhaps you have asked yourself and not been quite certain of the answer.

She said that when she started writing novels, the kind of straight novels which people like her would have written were very autobiographical, very self revelatory, the equivalent of the strip-tease on the page, and that it therefore suited her to write with the disguise of the genre form. It was a sort of armour between herself and the world. But also, she admitted, there was another, rather less grand reason; she likes reading crime fiction, and its easy to write what you enjoy.

My second question was to ask if she had any special readers in mind when she wrote her books? She said that she didn't particularly think of anyone when she was writing. She admitted that she was now aware that someone would read what she had written, and that might perhaps slightly affect the way she wrote, but in the beginning she'd never been certain that there would be any one, and that it was only after the third book had come out that she had begun to realise that she might have an audience.

What about the actual nitty gritty of writing? Could new writers learn anything from her about how to structure their day? She fits in her writing with other, various, commitments, including school holidays. She doesn't have a set pattern to her day, preferring to write at random; she thought she was not a particularly good example to follow. Although she knows she is a professional writer, yet she feels that her odd habit — writing for half an hour here and half an hour there, means that she doesn't think that perhaps her approach is professional enough. But that's how she feels happiest. Even though it can be difficult to pick up from where she left off she says it doesn't matter too much as she's never known what she was going to say until she'd said it, and she's never had a complete plan of her books in her mind.

From the structure of the day we moved to the structure of the book. Did she work carefully at her plots? Have an early synopsis? Know from the beginning how and where clues were to be planted?

I had some interesting revelations with this question. Jessica Mann pointed out that the problem with not having a plan and a programme to her day was that from one day to the next she never knew what she was going to say. There were an awful lot of days when she simply didn't know what was going to happen. She would love to have a structure, and every time she thought about writing a new book, she thought that this time she would manage one; she would do what other, real, authors did and have a chapter plan, a plot plan, a character list, and she would know what was going to happen, and then she would be able to sit down every day and write her five or ten pages and it would be no problem. But she simply couldn't do it; she never knew what was going to happen to whom, how, when, where and why. She didn't even know the characters. She often started with two people and a situation, would get terribly excited and write a chapter, a sort of scene setting chapter, and think 'brilliant' this time she knew what was going to happen. She would then wake up the next morning and have no idea how things were going to develop, so she would have to force her way on. The mystery as far as she was concerned, was that by the end of the book the whole thing appeared to be neatly and tightly plotted.

Having dealt with the structure of the books I then asked if she didn't think that characters dictated the way books would emerge?

She accepted that what mattered to her were the

characters and not the plot. She thought that crime writers could be divided into three categories, those who were interested in plot, those who cared about place, and those whose main interest lay in people; she was in the latter category.

Did she spend much time on research?

She admitted that on the whole she usually invented; though she had done some research for one of her books which was set in the nineteenth century.

Finally, I asked her if she had any tips she would like to pass on to the first time writer?

She said that when people asked her that question, she always quoted Ogden Nash: 'Apply seat of pants to seat of chair.' But seriously, she added, her advice would be to be much more professional about writing than she was. Writers ought to try and force themselves to get into the habit of writing a certain amount each day at a certain time. And they shouldn't try to write crime fiction unless it was what they liked reading.

Colin Dexter's love of crossword puzzles is reflected in his writing. His style has been called 'labyrinthine' and 'mandarin' and owes much to his desire to provide major complexities of plot. But it is not the intricate and closely woven plot that makes his work stand out from the more traditional detective story, with its Great Detective and his silent subordinate, it is the way that he makes his characters totally believable as he describes the world with which they interact. The clever insertion of clues and the brilliant description of motives are an added bonus.

The immediate reason why he took up crime fiction was that he took a crime story away with him on holiday and decided he couldn't do worse, and probably could write something much better! But his less obvious reason was that he had always been interested in the works of John Dickson Carr — the locked room type of mystery, as a boy. His great passion was that he always *liked to know the answer*. He had never taken to psychological books, because there was no puzzle element in them. What he liked best, which is why he was so fond of algebra, was for things to work out neatly and clearly. This interest had brought him to the crossword puzzle, which was one of his delights. There was always going to be a solution to a puzzle, and if he couldn't find it immediately then he would worry at it until he knew the answer. What Colin Dexter likes is a neat, conclusive ending; a solution which is good, interesting and perhaps surprising.

On the other hand he saw himself as communicating with the person sitting opposite on a commuter train. He wanted him to be so interested in what he was reading that he wouldn't be able to stop turning over the pages. He said that he was conscious that people had to be moved swiftly forward by the plot and that his objective would have been achieved if his reader was saddened that his journey had come to an end and there was no more time left for him to continue reading.

Colin Dexter's day tended to be somewhat different to that of Jessica Mann. Until recently he has had a full time job, and so has been unable to write during the day time. Even so, he admitted to not much of a structure. He got home around 6 o'clock, had some food, helped with the washing up, listened to the Archers, and then considered he was free for the rest of the evening. He worked between 8 and 9.30 when he would go out to his local for a pint of beer. Quite often on his return he would go back to his work and put in another longish stint. He tended to work most weekends. He found writing easy as it was something apart from his daily work, it got him outside himself. Now that he had retired he found it more difficult to get into writing. He had always tended to think haphazardly, when walking the streets, for instance. A stiff whisky helped to get him off to a good start!

His approach to the question of plot structure, as with Jessica Mann, was also flexible. He either started from one idea, or had a pretty good notion what would happen between A and Z. He certainly didn't think it crucial to have a rigid structure, because it was important to be able to have the possibility of having different endings. Some books began with one idea, others he knew where he wanted to go right from the beginning. He had learnt that if anything appeared to go wrong then it was useless to worry, you just had to jump over that particular river on your magic carpet. Faith

84

played a large part in the whole process. It was however important to start off with one good idea. He had also learnt that even though he might be writing rubbish it was best simply to continue and not to worry if something wasn't possible — it was easy, later, to find a solution to that particular problem. If you went on writing, rather than brooding, then by the very process of writing you would be able to get new ideas.

Did his characters dictate the format of his books? Colin Dexter thought that the actual writing process took over the book, and that if the characters were physically in one place only then did the author realise what could happen to them. Ideas sprang out of the writing itself, so that if you had various ingredients at the back of your mind, they would emerge as the writing flowed.

He admitted that he did little or no research. Occasionally he checks up with a pathologist to get some specific details right. What he tends to do is try not to get involved in technicalities. He never has his characters in a police station, which he's never been in. But he does do his research of Oxford; he looks at streets and buildings and their juxtaposition to each other. He isn't really interested in police procedure, he gets his information from other people's books.

Finally we came to my last question — did he have any useful hints for readers of this book? The biggest difficulty for any writer he acknowledged, was the start. The important thing was to ignore the blank pages and simply begin to write; it was irrelevant if what you were writing was rubbish, it could always be discarded. Don't worry, he also added, if you haven't got much of an idea, if you don't know how things are going to develop. Just take it for granted that your magic carpet will find some way over the difficulty. Never write with a medium with which you are not familiar; if you don't know how to type, then much of the time will be spent trying to work out the intricacies of the keyboard, and a lot of precious energy will be expended. Don't feel that you have to have some grand design, a small incident will be all you need. Writing crime fiction is about building with bricks.

The world of Peter Dickinson is a closed world whose inhabitants often have extraordinary and unusual characteristics. It is a world of fantasy which is yet so vividly described that the reader has utter faith in its existence. Despite the bizarre settings and strange situations the format of the novels is the classical detective story — there is a mystery (in the first five books Superintendent Pibble is the self effacing hero) which is solved through the detective's logical deduction of clues and a series of suspects each of whom is clearly a potential murderer. He is marvellously creative, so that long after his books have been read his extraordinary worlds remain to haunt the imagination.

As with the other writers, Peter Dickinson only liked to read crime fiction. He has always written poetry, 'of the old fashioned kind' and thought that he might become a poet. At the same time he found himself enjoying Michael Innes and Margery Allingham, and was asked to review detective novels for the journal on which he worked. Somehow, he says, he always knew that some time in the future he would write crime fiction — that he was not equipped to write novels. One day when he was in the middle of reviewing, he suddenly thought of some titles for books, saw a very vivid picture of a black man in a pin striped suit. He could, he thought transpose a tribe to a modern city, and cause the murder of one of the tribesmen to be solved partly by modern methods and partly by anthropological ones. He brooded over this scene for some eighteen months, and then suddenly decided he would start. He knew who would be murdered, but as suddenly, lost confidence. It was like a very bad nightmare, and the only way out appeared to be for him to start on something completely different which would help loosen the writing block. So he started writing a children's book (he is justly famous for these), and was able to return to his earlier draft. Both came out at the same time.

He feels he writes for himself. He thought that all successful books had a voice which was unique to them, and once the author had captured it, then he didn't have to worry any further; that was what unsuccessful books lacked. It didn't matter whether there was one particular person or two who were central to the book, the crucial part was to have some sort of voice, which could change from book to book, as different voices emerged. He said that he rather tended to have the same sort of male protagonist — a somewhat weedy scholar, who, he realised, reflected his dislike of macho characters. It wasn't that he minded tough heroes, and indeed, from the point of view of reader identification he thought it best to give his hero one magic gift with which he could defeat the world — it didn't matter what, any unlikely gift could be used — say brilliant computer know how. It was crucial not to cheat the reader, whose expectations should be of great importance to the writer.

Because Peter Dickinson is a full-time writer the structure of his day is different to both that of Jessica Mann and Colin Dexter. He sits down at his desk at 9.30 and works solidly through for three hours. He doesn't work on bank holidays or weekends. He says his writing may only consist of looking back on his previous chapters, but however his morning works out, he says it is crucial for him to have that discipline of the three hours. On a good day he can produce as much as one thousand words of his first draft.

Our third author also has a somewhat haphazard attitude to plot. He recounted the way he developed the plot of one of his favourite books, *King and Joker*. He thought it might be amusing to put the Royal Family at breakfast, and then have a practical joke played on them. He had a general idea that a murder would finally be committed, but he wasn't quite certain how this would come about. Other themes began to intrude, though he continued with the idea of the practical joke with which he was having an enjoyable time. The jokes themselves provided major clues, but they had to be looked at in the round rather than as separate events. As the book progressed, so he wrote down a few details, but not many.

He saw the question of characters in terms of development. A person would come into a room, and you then wrote about them. All fiction writing depended on a special kind of coherence; the author had to have that essential inventive grasp. Fiction was a game we all played, it was an imaginative stimulus which we were programmed to need. If the writer was on form then that imaginative coherence would build up of its own volition, if not, then he would have to make a conscious effort to think about it. He believed it was critical to think about the plot and about the world in which the characters found themselves, rather than just hoping that somehow you would get there by instinct. It was also important to imagine what people might be doing when they weren't on stage. Even with his more fantastic characters he thought that they worked because he had faith in their fantasies.

He believes in doing at least some research, even though many of his books have an imaginary setting. It is crucial to get the environment correct, and the ecology on which it is founded.

And what about good advice as to best practice? He said that he'd been very lucky in that he'd always had two hats: he was a writer of both children's books and of crime fiction. It gave variety to his life. He felt that it was a mistake to stick to the same characters all the time, they might be able to develop over five books, but then the chances were that they would lose their spontaneity. So it made sense to have more than one string to your bow. He also thought it important to discover the pace which suited you best. It was good to have a routine because it would get you through the bad patches. If you feel you want to stop writing, then you should feel free to do so. At the same time you should never over work in one day — that usually turned out to be counter productive. An essential ingredient of good writing was to believe in what you were writing, and to remember that your characters needed to have a life of their own outside the pages of your book. His final tip was that it was important never to believe that the reader doesn't notice details; this was quite untrue.

The description of Anthony Price's books which comes most readily to mind is elegant, original and tortuous. His plots, which so often reflect his interest in military history, (he writes about ancient and Roman Britain, the 1914-18 war, whatever he is researching at the time), are labyrinthian and gripping. The world of intelligence is depicted as a battle between good and evil, and his hero, Dr David Audley, is seen as a man of great complications but also of great simplicity, whose unusual past gradually emerges in the different volumes.

Anthony Price had never wanted to write murder stories; he thought they were too unpleasant. He has been a journalist most of his life and has had to cover murders and other crimes quite often, and has therefore felt no inclination to see them replicated in print. But he too, like Colin Dexter, has been caught up in a great passion — the study of espionage. He thought spying was both fascinating and outrageous, and there he was, living very much in the era of the spy, with Burgess and Maclean shaking his kind of world. He is a historian and knows a considerable amount about the Elizabethan age, when spying very much came into its own. What he has always wanted to dissect is the dividing line between patriotism and treachery, for he is convinced it is possible to be both a patriot and a traitor at one and the same time. To explore that sort of world was much more fun than the murky, and often boring, or so he thought, world of the murderer and his victim. Anyway, as he can't write to order, finds writing about people rather than working out intricate plots more interesting and also prefers reading about spies, the transition to examining the world of intelligence seemed natural.

His reply to my third question was somewhat individual-istic. He said that on the whole he wrote for himself, because he wanted to know how the book was going to end! He confessed that he didn't work out his plots in too great a detail, so that writing was a voyage of discovery. He was mostly interested in his characters and spent much time trying to find out what they were doing, but once he had come to grips with them, then his self interest went and his main objective was to discover what happened at the end, and this is what kept him writing on. Nowadays he also found himself writing for people who themselves had written in to him demanding to know what happened later to his characters, and why; in other words to those who had reacted to his work.

Anthony Price is the editor of the *Oxford Times* and has

no time during the week for any writing. He always works at weekends or when he has a day off. He says it takes him some time to get into the right frame of mind, so it is more cost effective to work for long stretches of time — about five hours, of which he reckons one is lost trying to recapture the previous mood. He too bribes himself with scotches — but then admits this can become less cost effective as his judgement can get flawed. On the credit side, he thinks that drink in moderation can release inhibitions, though that too can be dangerous!

He sees his characters as part of a repertory company; with each one needed to have people look at them in a different way. His books are about characters and their personalities. In his latest book he examined slightly flawed individuals. He said that he had what he called albums of people in mind; it was characters who made the plot not the other way round. The plot he saw as very much a flexible instrument which had a life of its own. Mystery was only a small part of his books, and he was perfectly happy to let the reader decide what happened next. The point was, that no one was ever right about anything; life was not a logical crossword. He certainly didn't consciously muddy the waters; individuals could put out theories which might well have been correct, even though in the end they turned out to have been wrong.

It was his firm opinion that it was the author who ran the book. But of course he could easily create characters who would do things which were anathema to him, such as, for instance, betraying their country. What was important was to play fair, and not, perhaps, getting rid of a character because he was proving inconvenient. It was also important to rein back a favourite character as he might well end up running the book, which would do it no good.

As we know, Anthony Price is fascinated by military history so finds research highly enjoyable. He likes to discuss his ideas with other people; he reads carefully, and finds that part of the process more fun than the writing.

His final message was not dissimilar to that of our other writers. You need to have words on paper, books don't write themselves. If you decide to write 200 words an hour then you will have set yourself some sort of target. It is useful to have a central idea, but what is more crucial is to see the characters clearly. Writing is hard work, it's difficult to get away from your book, so you need supportive people round you.

What conclusions can we reach from the advice of my four authors? First, it is quite clear that you, the first time writer of crime fiction, must have both a love of and an interest in the genre. Your imagination must already have been captured before you start writing.

Don't worry about particular readers, you don't have to have one in mind. What is important is for you to take your readers seriously. Don't cheat on them, and don't underestimate their intelligence.

As to how you structure your day; you must suit yourself and your own lifestyle. If you have a job then clearly it will be impossible for you to work during the day, and evenings might also prove difficult. But there is no doubt that, whatever pattern you impose on yourself, it has to be regular. All four authors spent a considerable amount of time working on their books. In other words, you have to be pretty dedicated if you want to be successful.

The question of plots produced interesting answers. Not one of the four spent much time in developing their plots, or thinking about their clues, or even working at their endings. However what was also clear is that they all agreed that there had to be a logical progression, the puzzle had eventually to fit neatly together. So if you see yourself as an imaginative and intuitive writer remember that that is only half the battle; you need a proper structure on which to base your approach.

And don't worry about your characters, take them as they come, but also keep a firm hold on them. Think about them in the round, see them surrounded by other people, in different settings, doing various things. Believe in them.

Always get your facts right. If you're not interested in police procedures then don't write about them. You can easily create your own world with its own rules — but make certain that the reader understands that that is what you have set out to do.

I hope that this chapter has given you some useful ideas as to how to set about writing. As you have seen, each author has his or her structure to the day, method of writing, way of creating plots and characters, so whatever your habits, you can set your own pattern. All that is important is that you believe in your own creation.

Chapter Ten

How to get published

We are now assuming that you have finished a book of crime fiction; your friends have encouraged you to get it published, and feeling confident that perhaps you might have a chance, you decide to look around you and see what the world has to offer.

But first a word about your typescript. There are certain formalities that you have to observe before any manuscript is ready to be sent to a publisher or an agent.

Your work should be typed on A4 paper (or the equivalent if you are using a word processor) of medium thickness, and with a 1½-2 inch margin on the left hand side. Double spacing has to be used throughout the typescript as it makes corrections, either by your editor or the copy editor, that much easier. Pages should be numbered throughout in a consistent manner.

Having prepared a manuscript which looks professional, what do you do next?

You choose either the agent or the publisher who you think might be interested in your work.

Let us presume that you don't want to send your work to an agent, you're not quite sure what they do, and you don't have any names to whom to send it. Look on your local library shelves to get some idea which publishers specialise in crime fiction. Ask the librarians, they will probably be able to tell you which publishers you ought to contact. Do *not* send your manuscript to the publisher who has recently published your favourite work of historical romance; the chances are that they specialise in that particular genre, and know little about crime fiction.

Look for a hardback publisher, as paperback publishers, on the whole, are not particularly interested in first novels.

Having chosen your publisher, what is your next step? What you do is send them a letter, preferably short, which simply states that you are enclosing a synopsis and the first three chapters of a book, called . . . This makes life both easier for the publisher (they don't have to have bulky typescripts littering their office desks) and easier for you, in that if you are having a professional copy of your book, then it can wait until you hear the outcome of the letter. If the publisher likes what he has read then he will ask you to send the rest of the typescript.

Remember to send return postage with your preliminary letter. If you don't then you will simply be reminded that you have not done so, or worse, your work may sit around for longer than you would have wished! Do not forget to keep a copy; even though you may have sent, and indeed I hope you do, your parcel recorded delivery, the Post Office is not infallible. A xerox of the first three chapters won't be too expensive.

So what happens next? I'm afraid that what happens next is that you wait. It is impossible to say how long a publisher may wish to keep your typescript. So much depends on how much is going through the office, whether, even at this stage, a second opinion might have been asked for; there are a lot of imponderables over which you have absolutely no control. Once you have received the publisher's acknowledgement of receipt of your manuscript there is nothing you can do but wait patiently.

However, if you have not heard from the publisher within two months then you are entitled to write in and ask how things are going. But remember to sound polite!

Suppose that your manuscript is rejected. What is your next step to be? If you are still determined not to send it to an agent then my advice would be to send it to another publisher. Remember that many an author has had well over ten rejections before they found a home for their work. The problem for you of course, is that you will probably have had very little information from the publishers as to why they are rejecting your typescript. You might well have been a marginal case, but that need not necessarily appear in their letter of rejection. You may by this time be somewhat despondent. Is this the time to try looking for an agent?

Where does one find agents, and what do they do? One finds them mostly in the *Writers and Artists Yearbook* which is not only a wonderful source of information about who is who in the business, but also gives you good advice on how to set about getting in touch with the people you have chosen. You will find that agents are listed alphabetically, and that under their name they will have a short description of the kind of work they specialise in.

Most agents state that they will accept full length manuscripts, what their charges are for handling your work, if there is a reading fee or not, if they give editorial advice.

What do agents do for their clients? Their main purpose is to look after the interests of their authors. This is done in a number of ways. If you are a first time author, and have been accepted by an agent, then the chances are that you may well be given some editorial advice. Most first attempts are not usually quite up to being sent to publishers, so do not be surprised if, despite the fact that you have been offered a contract, you find yourself having to do some considerable rewriting.

One additional word about finding your agent. You will see in the *Yearbook* that agents specify their interests. Take heed of this information. As with publishers, do not send your typescript to an agent who has clearly stated a preference for works of travel. You will have wasted both their time and yours. There is another reason for being careful who you pick; it is a good idea to go to agents who specialise in your field or who handle other authors who write in the same genre because they will be on good terms with the right editors and know not only where to place your book, but also what the going market rate is.

What else do agents do for their 10% fee? They might help you at an early stage of your manuscript once you have had your first book published — obviously it will be too late for them to help you out in the initial stages of your first work. Or, as I mentioned previously, suggest revisions. They will submit your manuscript to the appropriate editors.

There is some advantage for a first time author to be submitted to a publisher by an agent. Unsolicited manuscripts from unknown authors usually go into the general pool of a publisher's office, out of which they may find it difficult to emerge. If an agent sends in a manuscript then the editor will know that the work has already passed a major test — the author has been contracted by the agent who must obviously think he or she is good enough to come on the agent's list.

Suppose that the first publisher to whom the typescript is sent turns it down? Then it is up to the agent to send it on to the next one who they think might be interested. Again, this will be a faster process than might be possible with an unsolicited typescript.

Let us assume that the agent has found a publisher. What happens next? The author will find that the agent then deals with all the financial haggling that may go on; less embarrassing for the author who may or may not know what the going rate is, and may or may not have the wrong kind of expectations. The usual outcome can well be a higher advance than anticipated. Certainly the chances of getting a grip on rights, of whatever kind, are also good. An agent will generally split up the world market so that British publishers will have British and Commonwealth rights, and separate deals will be made over American and translation rights.

Subsequent to the contract being signed, an agent will always be the arbitrator between the publisher and the author over such thorny problems as, say, the design of the cover. They will also ensure that you are registered for Public Lending Rights — crime fiction is the second most popular category of fiction borrowed from public libraries.

Following the publication of your book an agent will check on all the royalty statements sent in by the publishers (which come about twice a year) and ensure that they are paid on time. They will also monitor sales and monies due, and of course will chase up for reprints where necessary, and ask for a reversion of the rights if a publisher decides not to reprint.

Your agent, like your editor, is there to listen, advise and often provide a shoulder to weep on. Sometimes they'll even take you out to lunch!

What do agents not do? In the first place they can't sell unsaleable work, and they won't want to. Neither can they teach you to write, they will only be interested in helping you with the revision process, and some agents, of course, may not wish to do this either.

Irrespective of whether you have gone through an agent or straight to a publisher, once your work has been accepted you will then be expected to help out in the process of its publication. The moment that proofs of your book are ready you will be sent them for correction. This is not the time to decide that you want a complete rewrite! Corrections are very expensive and, if extensive, may well have to be paid out of your own pocket. You should simply look for printer's errors. And once you have sent them back there is little else for you to do.

Your agent may or may not have persuaded the publishers to spend some money on your book for promotion purposes. On the whole a first novel is unlikely to have much spent on it. You may think this is a chicken and egg situation — if no money is spent, then how is the great British public going to be made aware of the excellence of your offering? At one level you're right. The publisher, on the other hand, will argue that it may well be money down the drain, and that it should only be spent once the author is established. But that's in the future. At the moment all you will be interested in is having your book placed. So settle down, and start writing.

Bibliography

The following titles from which the author has quoted, and some recommended reading, are listed in the order in which they appear in the book.

Whodunit? A guide to Crime, Suspense and Crime Fiction Edited by H. R. F. Keating (Windward)

A Catalogue of Crime Jaques Barzun & Wendell Hertig Taylor (Harper)

Writing Crime Fiction H. R. F. Keating (Black)

Bloody Murder. From the Detective Story to the Crime Novel Julian Symons (Faber)

A Kiss Before Dying Ira Levin (Michael Joseph)

The Honourable Schoolboy John Le Carré (Hodder & Stoughton)

Silver Blaze from *The Complete Short Stories of Sherlock Holmes* Arthur Conan Doyle (John Murray)

Sweet Danger Margery Allingham (William Heinemann)

Maigret Stonewalled Simenon (Penguin)

Murder in Mesopotamia Agatha Christie (Collins) Reproduced courtesy of Aitken & Stone

Death on the Nile Agatha Christie (Collins) Reproduced courtesy of Aitken & Stone

A Night of Errors John Appleby (Victor Gollancz) Reproduced courtesy of A. P. Watt

Enter a Murderer Ngaio Marsh (Collins)

Flowers for the Judge Margery Allingham (Heinemann)

The Case of the Abominable Snowman Nicholas Blake (Collins)

The Crooked Hinge John Dickson Carr (Hamish Hamilton)

The Murder of Roger Ackroyd Agatha Christie (Collins)

Singing in the Shrouds Ngaio Marsh (Cassell)

The Silent World of Nicholas Quinn Colin Dexter (Macmillan)

A Taste for Death P. D. James (Faber)

A Dark Adapted Eye Ruth Rendell (Century Hutchinson) Reproduced courtesy of A. D. Peters

A Fatal Inversion Barbara Vine (Viking) Reproduced courtesy of A. D. Peters

Smallbone Deceased Michael Gilbert (Hodder & Stoughton)

The King of the Rainy Country Nicholas Freeling (Victor Gollancz)

The Colour of Murder Julian Symons (Collins)

Not One of Us June Thomson (Constable)

No More Dying Then Ruth Rendell (Century Hutchinson)

The Last House Party Peter Dickinson (Bodley Head)

Plotting and Writing Suspense Fiction Patricia Highsmith (Poplar)

The Sweet Sickness Patricia Highsmith (William Heinemann)

People Who Knock On The Door Patricia Highsmith (Penguin)

A Helping Hand Celia Dale (Constable)

The Smooth Face of Evil Margaret Yorke (Arrow)

A Demon in My View Ruth Rendell (Century Hutchinson)

Funeral Sites Jessica Mann (Macmillan)

High Heels Miles Tripp (Macmillan)

The Parasite Person Celia Fremlin (Victor Gollancz)

Beast in View Margaret Millar (Victor Gollancz)

Impeccable People Elizabeth Fenwick (Victor Gollancz)

No Medals for the Major Margaret Yorke (Bles)

Farewell My Lovely Raymond Chandler (Hamish Hamilton)

The Maltese Falcon Dashiell Hammett (Picador)

The Doomsters Ross MacDonald (Collier-Macmillan)

A Catskill Eagle Robert Parker (Penguin) Reproduced courtesy of Murray Pollinger

Putting in the Boot Dan Kavanagh (Jonathan Cape)

Farewell My Lovely Raymond Chandler (Hamish Hamilton)

The Godwulf Manuscript Robert B. Parker (Penguin) Reproduced courtesy of Murray Pollinger

Dupe Sara Paretsky (Victor Gollancz)

Indemnity Only Sara Paretsky (Victor Gollancz)

Going to the Dogs Dan Kavanagh (Viking)

The Midnight Man Loren D. Estelman (Hale)
Blue City Ross MacDonald (Cassell)
King's Ransom Ed McBain (Hamish Hamilton)
All on a Summer's Day John Wainwright (Macmillan)
All Through the Night John Wainwright (Macmillan)
Gideon's Art J. J. Marric (Hodder & Stoughton)
Killer's Wedge Ed McBain (Penguin)
Gideon's Day J. J. Marric (Hodder & Stoughton)
The Late Mrs D Hillary Waugh (Victor Gollancz)
The Taste of Proof Bill Knox (Longman)
The Sunday Hangman James McClure (Macmillan)
Nerve Dick Francis (Michael Joseph)
The Danger Dick Francis (Michael Joseph)
Flying Finish Dick Francis (Michael Joseph)
Puppet on a Chain Alistair MacLean (Collins)
Triple Ken Follett (MacDonald)
Judas Country Gavin Lyall (Hodder & Stoughton)
Travelling Horseman Nicholas Luard (Weidenfeld & Nicolson)
The Vivero Letter Desmond Bagley (Collins)
Checkmate David Brierley (Collins)
A Kind of Anger Eric Ambler (Bodley Head)
Comes the Dark Stranger Harry Patterson (Long)
Smiley's People John Le Carré (Macmillan)
Tomorrow's Ghosts Anthony Price (Victor Gollancz)
The Inscrutable Charlie Muffin Brian Freemantle (Jonathan Cape)
The Secret Lovers Charles McCarry (Century Hutchinson)
The Endless Game Bryan Forbes (Collins)
The Human Factor Graham Greene (The Bodley Head)
  Reproduced courtesy of Laurence Pollinger Ltd.
The Striker Portfolio Adam Hall (William Heinemann)
The Warsaw Document Adam Hall (William Heinemann)
Consequence of Fear Ted Allbeury (Collins)
The Endless Game Bryan Forbes (Collins)
The Miernik Dossier Charles McCarry (Century Hutchinson)
Funeral in Berlin Len Deighton (Jonathan Cape)